Moving Up
Action Steps for
Career Success

E. Anne Tipper

Dedication

To all the many men and women who, through their presence in my life, have taught me the lessons I am able to share here with others.

Acknowledgements

Thank you to my editors, both official and unofficial, who read through my drafts and gave their feedback, helping to shape this book into more than what it was: Mark Tipper, Yvonne Gonzales, Sue Malone, Connie Tooman, Suzanne Deshchidn from srdediting.com, and Lindsay Christensen.

To my parents, Sue Malone & Michael Tooman, who challenged me to think for myself and create solutions while providing a safe place for me to discover.

To my Home Depot family who helped shape many of my professional skills and tools and were the testers of my many activities and ideas.

And to my husband, who has supported me through the entire process.

Table of Contents

Introduction

Enjoy reading. Let me know what you think or if you have questions. A few items of note to explain the icons in the book:

 an idea, suggestion or activity

 a written activity

 a full page downloadable worksheet is available; see Appendix for access

 additional detailed information can be found in the corresponding chapter

Enjoy!
Anne Tipper

SECTION ONE

The Basics

Chapter One

The Golden Ticket

Over the course of my career my position was eliminated or restructured six times. Yet with all of the restructures I came through with a new job every time and all but one a promotion. How did I do it? What was my secret? There are several but one I will elaborate here:

I had a Golden Ticket.

What is a Golden Ticket? A Golden Ticket allows freedom in the job. A Golden Ticket gives more opportunities. A Golden Ticket creates a safer haven in restructures and downsizing or at least gives a leg up.

Receiving a Golden Ticket

Before becoming eligible for a Golden Ticket the basics of the job must be covered: Consistently arrive at work on time and complete the job; get along with others but don't socialize to the point it hurts productivity; be professional. All of these still do not earn a Golden Ticket. So, in a nutshell, the only way to get a Golden Ticket is....

☑ Check off the boss's boxes first.

No matter how trivial the request might seem, no matter if it does not appear to be the right use of time, if there is no idea why the request has been made, and even if it means your list goes unfinished that day, it doesn't matter. Check off the boss's boxes first. Because when their directives have been satisfied trust is built and freedom is given in return.

Realistic
Estimations:
Unrealistic
Deadlines

Caution: There are times when a request will not allow a critical project to be complete. In these cases, discuss the request with the boss and explain what will happen if their request is completed. Many times they are not aware of everything in process and most times will adjust their request or bring in additional resources. It is important not to question everything. Common sense must determine if the request is unreasonable.

When I was a buyer for flooring I worked with a senior merchant. The senior merchant was much more knowledgeable than I, had much more experience, contacts, you name it. He was an expert in his field. I was new to the position and was learning tremendously as I went along. We both reported to the same boss. There were always some random projects requested of us. They didn't all make sense, but I ensured mine were always completed and turned in on time, if not early. My partner did not. I had no issues with my boss what-so-ever and was able to create all sorts of programs as a result. I was not micromanaged but instead given pretty much free reign, even being new to the position. Interestingly enough, my partner was constantly at odds with our boss. He did not agree with the direction given, or the project, or the achievables, or the trivial tasks. I did not know who was right, I did not possess enough knowledge at the time to make an informed opinion, but I did know, that once I completed my boss's requests, I was given freedom. I received: a Golden Ticket.

The flip side of a Golden Ticket is frustration on both sides. The boss does not understand why the subordinate will not do what is requested. The subordinate is frustrated because all their hard work goes unnoticed.

Early in his career, my husband was working for a big box retailer. He has always had an eye for how to position product for great sell-through, and would adjust product locations creatively. There was, of course, a list of items to do from his boss and he would get most of them executed with a few taking a little longer to finish while he completed some of his own ideas. His boss honed in on only the items unexecuted and saw nothing of my husband's efforts. My husband was frustrated. Sales would be moving up in the areas he adjusted, but he received absolutely no credit for his effective entrepreneurialism. One day his boss, out of frustration, said something like: "Damn it, Tipper, why can't you just do what I ask you to do?!" An "Ah Ha" moment occurred. My husband realized his boss could not see past the unaccomplished request. Going forward, my husband checked off his boss's list first, and then moved on to creative merchandising.

Overnight, he became a hero. Nothing had changed except the order in which the tasks were accomplished. By doing what his boss asked first he received a Golden Ticket.

Golden Ticket Process

Now as simple as it sounds, there is some fine print:

A Sense of Urgency

- ✓ Complete quickly
- ✓ If not feasible, complete prior to the deadline

Follow Up / Communication

- ✓ Follow up prior to being asked for a progress update
- ✓ Always communicate when a task or directive has been completed

Outcome / Additional Info

- ✓ Give the boss the outcome of the project
- ✓ Keep the boss informed of any additional information learned along the way

Keep Communication Short and to the Point

- ✓ Update in outline form or quick bullet points
- ✓ Ideally in email or other trackable format

Losing a Golden Ticket

A Golden ticket can also be lost. The moment the boss's boxes stop being checked off, the ticket starts being handed back. And pretty soon, it is gone. Then the work begins all over again to earn it back.

What happens when inundated with requests and there is no possible way to complete all in the time allotted? Communicate with the boss. Have the list of tasks, explain how long each will take, and ask for their priorities. Let them make the decision on how to rank the tasks and assign new complete times, or rearrange resources so that all can still be completed. At the same time as bringing problems, have a solution in mind so if they do not have a ready answer, a suggestion is ready.

Be a Solver

Benefits

When restructures occur, or downsizing, or even promotions are available, the ticket holder comes to the forefront because they are reliable. They have the reputation of getting things done because the boss's requests have been accomplished. They are highly regarded. During succession planning meetings their name rises to the top. They are asked to join teams and gain exposure to more people. They have more opportunities, especially during restructures or when promotions become available. It is not a guarantee, but having a Golden Ticket definitely creates an advantage.

The Fine Print Exercise

Let's see if a Golden Ticket was handed out last week. Think back and list every task/project/request from the boss and write it down along with the date requested, and the due date if one was given. Now answer the following questions:

- ✓ Was it completed?

- ✓ Date complete – was it on time? Was it early?

- ✓ Who followed up first?

- ✓ Did you give any anecdotal information?

- ✓ How did you follow up? What was the communication vehicle?

- ✓ Communication length – how long did it take the follow up communication to occur?

Golden Ticket Review			
		Week of: _____	

Date Rec'd		Task/Project	

Due Date/Time	Complete?	Date/Time	Diff
	Y N		

Follow Up?	Comm Vehicle	Comm length?	Anecdotal info?
Me Boss			

Notes	

Future Tracking

Now do the same exercise but in real time, starting next week. Fill out the form (or create a note using a smart device or notepad) throughout this next week. Write every request down and monitor how quickly each is accomplished. It is amazing how quickly behavior can change when it is monitored.

Follow Up

Create a follow up mechanism to ensure the boss's requests are accomplished first. If in an office environment use a calendar or a To Do list, or use a smart phone to capture. If electronic devices are not allowed on the job a simple notepad can work well. The important point is to create a process so requests never fall through the cracks.

Summary

One of the quickest ways to earn freedom and job security is to check the boss's boxes first, and then complete your own. While doing so, keep these rules in mind to earn a Golden Ticket.

- ✓ Do the job well

- ✓ Have a sense of urgency

- ✓ Be the first to follow up

- ✓ Communicate the outcome and any pertinent additional information

- ✓ Keep communication short and to the point

Chapter Two

Be Approachable

Not All are Born Approachable

Some people are gifted with charisma and charm. Some people are innately welcoming and everyone likes them. Some people are natural extroverts and truly enjoy and gain energy from being around others. These people tend to make friends easily and lead groups, even when they were small children. They do not have to cultivate the skillsets of approachability. But many people have to *learn* how. And if in the former category where this comes easy, read on in case the need arises to help others in developing skill sets that you possess effortlessly.

Now me, I am not one of those gifted people. I have had to work on this area my entire life. As a child, I was always a bit shy and introverted. Of course, as with most shy people, once I got to know someone I was very engaged and open and chatty, but that initial time where I did not know anyone, or walked into a new classroom or event, it was difficult at best. I was more than happy to be on the outskirts of a situation where I could watch what was happening and wait until others approached and invited me to participate.

In high school, I was involved in sports and then later became a cheerleader. Interesting enough, I was still shy. I could turn on the exuberance when needed, but inside was still unsure and insecure, which unfortunately, was interpreted as being stuck up and too good for others. The perception of others was that since I was in a socially visible position with an assumedly outgoing personality the onus was on me to be friendly and welcoming to everyone else. So I had to push myself beyond my own comfort zone and initiate communication. Others assume this is natural for me, but I have had to make a conscious effort to do so. The saying "fake it until you make it" worked for me. Although at first an act, I was able to gain the confidence and ability to initiate communication rather than waiting for others to do so.

Expectations in the Workplace

As I began to move through my career, especially as a manager, I found myself in similar circumstances. Position means different things to different people but the higher position the more others wait to allow you to initiate conversation, to see if you welcome them, to see if you are open to them.

I had a reputation at Home Depot for being a tough manager. I was very knowledgeable, did my homework before I arrived and had an uncanny way of finding little details that others missed. I could quickly assess a situation and drill down to the heart of a matter. This could be very intimidating on the receiving end. It was crucial to set the tone and introduce myself, ask questions of others, and put them at ease as much as possible. It didn't matter that I was introverted and tended to be shy. No one cared. In fact, most people had no idea; how could I be shy given the position I held?

One of the division presidents I worked under was also shy. He oversaw twelve states, 100,000 employees and multiple officers of the company. He was extremely successful in his career and was brilliant. I thought very highly of him and still do. While in stores, I would hear people talk about how he didn't really talk to people and since he was the president he should be more outgoing. I would come to his defense, since I knew him well, and let people know he was just shy. Again, no one cared. "He is the president," they said, "it doesn't matter if he is shy, it's his job."

On the opposite end of the spectrum, even in entry level positions, it is important to be approachable. If a person is closed and does not initiate conversations or get to know new people, they are less likely to be noticed for promotion. Come review and raise time, managers do not remember those who blended into the background. Instead, make a positive impression. The approachable person is asked out to lunch where relationship building and networking occur. The approachable person is considered a team player if there is no other reason to doubt it. The approachable person is more often given the benefit of the doubt on work ethic, competence, abilities unless proven otherwise. It is not just for managers to be approachable, but for everyone who wants to excel in their positions. If a person is unapproachable, they may miss out on help that otherwise would have been forthcoming.

When I was the merchandising secretary, my first and entry level position with Home Depot, I supported the entire merchandising department. I was the only position to have a computer so typed up all correspondence and projects for the department. Supporting over forty people, I became very adept at reading almost every handwriting imaginable. But while I was learning, I would have to go back to the writer, ask questions, and have them proof the document.

Some of the people I supported were very welcoming, while others did not have time for a lowly merchandising secretary's questions, even though it was a project for them. Guess what happened with the projects of those that were unapproachable? I would do the best I could and send out their communications. Most of the time I got it right, but sometimes there was an error. Because those people were unapproachable, I was less inclined to go the extra mile to ensure their projects were perfect. The merchant assistants were not managers, they were not high level positions, but it was still important for them to be approachable. No matter the level of position in an organization, cultivating approachability towards all people is essential. Subordinates have the power to help or hinder a career, and one never knows who will become the boss. Kindness and respect will pay future dividends.

Later in my career, when I was the Regional Director of Operations, those who reported directly to me would sometimes not communicate when they needed help. When I asked them why, the response was "you are so busy and I didn't want to bother you." They were right, I was extremely busy, but it was my job to ensure they had the resources needed to be successful. So I created monthly check-ins to cover the status of their area and find out what they needed from me.

As a boss, no matter what you think, others are gauging you and your expressions, seeing if your actions match your words. They are waiting for you to set the tone. Go the extra mile to be approachable, back up words with actions, and show that you are open to them.

Cultivating Approachability

Approachability Research

Do a little research, whether over the next few days or a week, or from memory. Identify the people in your life (work place or personal), that you would consider approachable. Next, watch them. What is it that makes you perceive them as such? List the specific characteristics and behaviors. It is very important to capture tangible behaviors, those that can be emulated, not generalities.

For example, one could say an approachable person is friendly, which is a characteristic (and a good start), but go deeper, go to the root of why that person is approachable. What specifically do they do that creates friendliness? Do they smile a lot? Do they ask you about events to see how they went? Do they acknowledge you every time they see you? Do they look you in the eye? Those are specific, tangible actions that can be emulated. Get that granular in compiling the list.

Approachable Person		
Characteristic		
Specifics of Characteristic	Own?	Add?

Unapproachability research

Simultaneously, or after, think of people you find unapproachable. Same exercise – watch them. What specific actions does that person do that creates the perception of unapproachability? Again, be specific. For example, if you were to state "they seem closed off," that is a good start. Then ask "Why?" "How?" What are the specific actions they do that cause them to appear closed off? Are their arms crossed? Are they frowning? Do they neglect eye contact? Do they ignore you? Make a list of the specific actions.

Unapproachable Person			
Characteristic			
Specifics of Characteristic		Own?	Remove?

With the lists compiled, go through and look to see how many of the specific characteristics apply to you. How many of the specific actions on the approachable list can be incorporated into your style? Do you have any on the unapproachable list? What actions can be taken to mitigate the negative behaviors?

Peer Feedback

Take it one step further: get feedback from peers, direct reports, the boss, even family and friends may be able to give insight. In soliciting feedback, make sure to get specifics just as in the exercise above. Concepts are difficult to work with. Specifics are needed to either start incorporating into your style or work on eliminating.

Ways to be Approachable

Along with what has already been compiled from the previous exercises, here are some additional ideas to help develop approachability. While determining which activity and behaviors to incorporate into your style, be sure to be genuine. People can tell the difference.

 Make it a point to greet people first, say hello, shake hands if appropriate, and maintain eye contact with a smile.

 Learn people's names and use their names when saying hello. If it is hard to remember names, say their name several times if the first time meeting. Make notes on a smart phone to reference until remembering.

 Smile and keep eye contact with people while greeting them. When saying hello without looking, it comes across as a perfunctory gesture without meaning. Even if the hello lasts only a few moments, make it real.

 When receiving a phone call have a happy, welcoming voice. My father, whenever I would call and to this day, would always be happy to hear my voice and it made me feel welcomed. I learned from him what a difference tone makes when answering a call. Even if frustrated, irritated, interrupted, with almost no time, have a welcoming tone when answering the phone. If there is truly no time to talk, then don't answer the phone. If answering, keep your tone open and friendly. Many of us give tonal cues of frustration which communicate more than words.

 Ask people how their weekend, vacation, event was – but only if genuine. It is better to say nothing than ask a question by rote and not care or remember the answer.

 Ask people to lunch, coffee, or a quick bite after work. Many people are not comfortable initiating. Get to know them, create networking, find out amazing interests, hobbies, and skillsets that would never be known otherwise.

 Compliment people when genuinely impressed with something. It could be as simple as saying, "nice suit," but it is very important to be sincere.

 Congratulate people on achievements and accomplishments. Be specific on what the congratulation is for and any additional details to add more "umph" to the congratulations. Use their name when congratulating, maintain eye contact, and smile.

 Remember birthdays with a quick note, card, or call. With today's technology it is so easy to calendar reminders and drop a note.

Strive for a consistent upbeat mood. Moodiness creates an unapproachable person. My husband worked for a manager where one never knew what mood he would be in, whether one should go hide in their department or if he would be approachable that day. They even had a code word the first person that interacted with him would say over the intercom of the retail store to give everyone a heads up. So to be approachable, be consistent in treating colleagues, peers, direct reports, anyone working alongside. No matter what is going on personally or how frustrating a meeting was, or an interaction with a customer, put on filters and treat everyone consistently. Of course this is easier said than done, but to start, strive for consistency. Be mindful of the mood broadcasted and it will become easier.

Gauging Approachability

First, doing the research exercise explained previously should give a good idea of where you stand on approachability. If you have quite a few of the unapproachable characteristics and behaviors seen in others, it is a pretty good sign that you are perceived in the as unapproachable as well.

Second, be observant. Watch how others act around you:

- ✓ Do people tend to shy away or walk right up to you?

- ✓ Do people say hello with a follow up on how the weekend or vacation was? Or do they keep it to the bare minimum of social expectations?

- ✓ Are you invited to functions (birthday parties, lunch, a quick break) or does everyone wait for you to make the invitations?

- ✓ Are you left alone at gatherings or is there always someone that will come up and start a conversation?

- ✓ Do you invoke fear and nervousness in people without knowing why?

Managing Approachability

On the flip side, one can be so approachable that people lose respect for one's time. Instead of checking to see if another person has the time, they assume and interrupt. I briefly worked for a newly promoted manager who worked so hard to be approachable that she answered every question on the spot. She quickly gained the reputation of completing whatever was brought to her right away and became swamped with requests, overwhelmed, and unable to prioritize. She stepped down from the position only months into receiving it. She was unable to get her job done because she did not set boundaries.

If accomplishing tasks becomes difficult because of constant interruptions, being approachable is not an issue. What is a concern is that no boundaries have been established. If changing overnight would cause problems make gradual adjustments, where approachability can be maintained while gaining more time without interruptions. It is important to set boundaries, so if one needs something, acknowledge them, give direction (e.g., "as soon as I am finished with this, I will take a look and get back with you"; or "I am busy until 2pm, do you have time then?"), then continue with the current task. Ideally, set expectations of when open times are, although depending on the job that can be difficult. Do not be so approachable that it becomes impossible to strategize the day, prioritize actions, and accomplish the items that make you as well as your team successful.

Boundary Setting

 Be observant of those who are approachable, but not interrupted all the time. How do they do it? How have they safeguarded their time? How is it known when a good time is to approach them versus not? Start making a list and incorporate.

Consider requests, then based on priority give people a response timeframe. Immediate response, while necessary in some cases, can create a state of approachability that may not be maintainable.

 If people come up to chat at a bad time, acknowledge them, then let them know you are right in the middle of a project and ask if they are available later. Alternately, ask them if they would like to go to lunch, or meet for break.

 Establish an open time, similar to a college professor who publishes office hours.

 If working in an office or a cubicle with a door, close it when uninterrupted time is needed.

 Block out time on the calendar and go to an office or conference room with the door closed for a set period of time.

 Ask people to email requests, concerns, and ideas so they can be reviewed when more time is available to give the topic the focus it deserves. Listen to them, but refrain from giving away more time than can be afforded at that moment.

 Establish protocol: if you have an assistant, ensure people go through her/him prior to coming in your office. Be sure to have time to visit with people so they still have access to you unstructured.

 Establish a routine that is published or communicated to your staff. For example: Be unavailable until after 10am each morning to allow time to review and prep, and make any calls, or attend meetings required.

Summary

Approachability, including the right measure, is the responsibility of every person individually to create for themselves, no matter where one falls in the hierarchy of a company or career.

1.   Cultivate approachability by watching others both successful and unsuccessful in this endeavor. Emulate the positives and work to adjust conduct unbecoming.

2.   Ensure boundaries are in place to safeguard time while still remaining approachable.

Chapter Three

The Eleventh Hour Crisis

What is the Eleventh Hour Crisis?

When I supported the Vice President of Merchandising, one of my responsibilities was to coordinate the Open to Buy Day where potential vendors showed their products to the buyers. My assistant asked me to let her handle the process and to trust that she would take care of it without following up with her on progress. The Friday that all communication was to go out to the potential vendors, I had still not received any updates, nor had I seen any communication go out. It was 4pm. I asked my assistant for a status update and learned that not only was the project incomplete, she would be unable to complete it by the deadline. At this point there were over a hundred and fifty letters to write and send within an hour in order to be in the vendors' hands by 5pm Friday night. Even if we could make it, most would have already left their offices and unable to make travel arrangements until the following week.

Both my assistant and I created the Eleventh Hour Crisis.

My assistant: Communicating the impossibility of meeting a deadline without enough time to create a viable solution to rectify the situation.

Me: Allowing the project to progress without updates.

A manager cannot help their subordinates or ensure execution of a directive if they are not in the loop of roadblocks or circumstances along the way that preclude a successful outcome.

Why Does it Happen?

There are many reasons the Eleventh Hour Crisis occurs. Here are some of them:

- ✓ Conflict avoidance

- ✓ Poor planning and execution

- ✓ Unwillingness to become or admit to a perceived failure

- ✓ Overestimating capacity

- ✓ Procrastination

- ✓ Fear of disappointing others

- ✓ Lack of correct prioritization

- ✓ Poor Follow up

Instead of dealing with, resolving, or planning for the issues above, failure results. Others are not given the opportunity to bring in resources or ideas to save the project. Credibility is lost. Unable to deliver what was promised results in loss of trust. The ability to ascertain when future plans will not work is called into question. It can appear selfish—caring more about personal fears than ensuring the completion of the goal and success of the team.

Avoiding the Crisis

Be Aware of Reality

Take the time to realistically estimate the needs and timing of the project or goal in the first place and communicate the findings up front.   Agreeing to unknown timeframes, resources, or capabilities before researching to determine the achievability of the goal is foolish and will, more often than not, result in failure. Instead, ask for time in order to review and ensure the feasibility of the requirements.

6

Realistic Estimations

Schedule Project Time

Schedule time on the calendar to work on the project. The sooner work begins the sooner it can be determined if the project is on track or if there are roadblocks that will need to be dealt with. Procrastinating only exacerbates problems.

Schedule Regular Updates

Throughout the project, ensure the boss and colleagues receive updates on the status. Updates can be as simple as a quick email stating everything is on target, to setting up a time to meet to discuss details and roadblocks. The size and complexity of the project will determine the frequency or detail of updates with more complex and far-reaching projects needing more updates.

When there is a Potential Crisis

Communicate

Communicate as soon as there is the potential for being unable to deliver the project or assignment in the timeframe allotted. Some suggested points to include in the communication:

1) The reason – i.e. the roadblock, new information, change in resources

2) The solution to rectify the situation – which can possibly include:

12

Be a Solver

✓ shifts in resources: are there those that might be able to help? Can resources be pulled temporarily from one project (whether equipment, labor, money) in order to complete this one

✓ updated timeframe

✓ adjustment of the end result or project itself

✓ Re-prioritizing: is there a balance of work that can be adjusted, other work that can be postponed

3) Next steps – once an agreement has been made about what will happen, make sure to create the next steps and communicate to all involved.

A client of mine had various off-site meetings that she and her staff attended. Thirty minutes prior to the start of the meeting one of her directors called to let the Executive Director know he was unable to attend the meeting because of illness. Unfortunately, thirty minutes was not enough time to drive to the offsite meeting, much less find a replacement. This crisis could have been resolved if the call was made earlier, better yet, if the ailing Director found a replacement and simply communicated the change to the Executive Director.

The people you work with, whether those in authority, investors, colleagues on a project team, bosses, whomever, want an update or answer, not a problem dumped in their laps. They are looking to you to find a viable solution to the obstacle.

Ask for Help

Sometimes the answer is simply to ask for help. This can be tough because it shows we are human. Women especially try to do it all based on the fear of perception. It may feel that if a woman does not take care of everything herself she looks less than capable. That asking for help will be perceived as being lazy, inconsiderate, incompetent, self-centered, unaware of the job, disorganized, time challenged, unprofessional, that somehow the lack is inside. The true failure is not understanding when help is needed.

Partner

Partnering can be as simple as opening up to someone and explaining the dilemma. Ask for an opinion, or any ideas they may have. Many times someone looking from the outside can be more objective and suggest an idea or avenue that a person in the middle of the situation has overlooked. It might be using a time saving app or connecting with a person that has already done a portion of the work for another project that can be used for yours; or they may offer to help.

Delegate

Are you holding on to control too tightly? Are there others that can take on some of the work? Take a look at what can be given to others that would enhance their job, give them a stretch assignment, or just utilize their skillsets.

It is important to remember that asking for help goes both ways. When others are in need, it is important to contribute your time and ideas as well.

Own up to Mistakes

Others are much more willing to help those who own up to their shortcomings and inabilities, especially when the outcome was foretold. Making mistakes is an essential part of career development, as long as it contributes to future knowledge base. The pursuit of perfection leads to rigidity; the more risk avoidant, the more blinded to mistakes. Perfection-minded people tend to blame others and try to foist the responsibility of failure on someone else. People tend to be reluctant to help perfectionists. Instead, own up to mistakes and be as upfront as possible. State:

1) your mistake right up front

2) how it will affect the outcome of the project

3) what will be done differently

4) the solution or ideas to rectify

5) what needs to happen in order to move forward

Depending on the appropriateness of the situation, include what was learned from the experience and how it will change decision making going forward. Peers and bosses alike will want to know there is an understanding of what went wrong, how it affected the outcome, and what the plans are to move forward.

Recognizing and communicating when there is a problem, asking for help, and owning up to mistakes actually *increases* credibility and enhances a boss's view of abilities. Managers have a positive view of those that understand what they did and how it affected the outcome and then proceed to rectify the situation. They can trust that in future situations this individual will recognize when a project goes awry, will have a plan, and be able to handle it.

Learn From the Situation

Apply the new information learned to the next project. Many people are so thankful to just get past the hurdle or failed project they promptly forget what attributed to the problem in the first place and end up repeating the behavior. Take time after the fact to determine what caused the miss and put processes in place to mitigate those causes in the future.

List Out what Derailed the Project.

What could have changed the outcome? What actions could have been taken, or organizational change, or change in priority, communication, would have made it achievable? Just the act of writing these down can help in future projects. Don't stop at the first obvious answer, try to get at least three, ideally five, adjustments or changes that are impactful. Taking the time to go beyond the first ideas can bring "Ah Ha" moments that may not have normally been discovered.

Eleventh Hour Crisis

Project

Issue

Why?

What could have changed the outcome?

Create a Memory Maker

If there was something specific that caused the project to go sideways, create a saying, cartoon, or special code word to post at your desk as a reminder.

Summary

The best avenue is to avoid the Eleventh Hour Crisis to begin with:

1. Have realistic estimations
2. Schedule project time
3. Communicate status updates on projects along the way

Communicate as soon as it is discovered that a project, goal, or directive will not be accomplished in the designated timeframe or with the designated resources. It can be the difference between success and failure. Be prepared to suggest a solution demonstrating that not only is there awareness of the issue, but also an answer to the problem. With enough notice, workloads can be adjusted, additional resources brought in, or adjustment of scope created.

Don't be afraid to ask for help and own up to mistakes. Create more credibility by pro-actively communicating needs and shortcomings rather than trying to hide them. Waiting until the last minute creates a no win situation, causes frustration and failure, and reduces professional status. Tackle roadblocks head on and avoid the Eleventh Hour Crisis altogether.

Chapter Four

Attitude is Everything

The Effects of Attitude

Successful people are positive in the face of challenge, take set-backs as a growth opportunity, and turn their disappointments into energy that fuels their next opportunity. Successful people, no matter what comes their way, forge a path to accomplish their goals. And the opposite holds true as well. Those that have a negative attitude create their own self-fulfilling prophecy.

Experience, knowledge base, and social circles are not the most important aspects of moving forward in a career. Those, of course, help and are factors but the most crucial part of the puzzle is how a person handles setbacks, disappointments and even success. I have known brilliant people that struggled to get promoted because they had a discouraging attitude or were overly triumphant and shoved any success they achieved in others' faces. Conversely, everyone can name someone who continued to be rejected, turned down, looked over, but their can-do attitude eventually prevailed. They did not give up.

I was conducting final interviews for two positions that were open. After selecting the final candidate, there were two people that were not chosen. Both had interviewed for the same job previously and not been selected. It was very interesting to watch the different reactions between the two. One, I will call John for this example, became very bitter and upset that he was not chosen. John thought he was ready and felt it unfair to be looked over yet again. Even though his direct boss explained what he needed to accomplish in order to be selected, John's attitude stayed negative and his performance declined. As a result, this precluded him from future openings and made it much harder for him to be promoted.

The other individual, I will call him Stewart, took a completely different route. Although he was very disappointed and a bit demoralized after the second rejection, he took some time to school his emotions. He questioned why he did not receive the position, and what he still needed to do in order to be more qualified for the next opening. Stewart took it upon himself to expand out of his current role and learn more aspects of the business. He began taking on more of a leadership role with his peers and offered his time to train new people. When the next promotion became available, Stewart earned the promotion due to his positive attitude and effective self-development. It was impressive how he handled himself. Stewart went through the same tough situation as John, but Stewart used the opportunity to demonstrate his maturity. He improved his skillsets and prepared himself to be ready for the next opportunity.

John decelerated his career momentum based on his attitude and resulting actions, whereas Stewart's promotion was based on his attitude and the abundance of his positive actions. Stewart used the energy from his disappointment to fuel change rather than allowing it to drag him down.

A few months after Stewart's promotion I checked in with him to see how he was doing. He loved his job, was doing fantastic and actually appreciated not being chosen originally. Once in the position he understood how much he had to learn and was much more prepared for the new responsibilities because he had waited and developed himself more. No one wants to be set up to fail.

So how does one keep a positive attitude in the face of adversity? In the face of disappointment or an unfair ruling? Or when everything seems to be falling apart? How to become the Stewarts of the world and not the Johns?

I was having a particularly tough time and reached out to my father as a sounding board. To be completely honest, I reached out so he could join me in a pity party. Instead of feeding into my misery he quite pointedly said,

> "Anne, there is a silver lining in this."

> "No, there isn't, not this time." I replied, irritated with such a cliché response.

> "There is always a silver lining," he responded, "*It is your job to find it.*"

It is your job to find the silver lining, the positive movement, the good that will come out of the situation that you can create. That is the answer and the path to always having a good attitude towards just about anything that can come. Attitude is rarely objective, but a subjective tool to sway a person or the perception of a situation either positively or negatively. If always looking for positive outcomes, solutions, and outlooks, a person cannot help but be positive because that is the focus. The reverse is also true. If only the negative is seen, the cons, the rumors of untold tragedy, then that is what will be found. Energy goes towards the focus.

The Positive Path Process

Step One: Acknowledge the Present

8

Emotional
Strength

It is important to see clearly what is happening in the present in order to move on to the future. Create a list of pros and cons regarding the situation. Then, if needed, acknowledge having been hit with a setback or having been hurt. Allow the emotions time to grieve if needed, to validate, and then begin to heal.

Now look at the list of cons. Why did they occur in the first place? Is there something to be learned from the situation to change outcomes going forward? Is there a cause and effect that can be altered for the future? There may be cons that must be accepted and released, but be sure to look at what can be learned from the situation.

Step Two: List the Positives

Although Step One was to create a pro and con list, many times the cons are much longer because those are the items that stand out the most.   Revisit the exercise and list every positive possible, no matter how trivial or silly it seems.   Focus on how to turn the situation into an advantage or stepping stone to a better future. Try to write down at least ten positives, but keep going if more ideas can be added.   The objective is to start shifting perspective to how the situation can be changed, gain a positive spin and turn it into an advantage.

Many times others will have additional ideas. Brainstorming increases the pool of ideas enhancing the possibilities.

Positive Brainstorm

Situation:

Positives	Actions

Step Three: Attitudinal Action

The next step is using the positive viewpoint to create attitudinal action. It is not enough to simply have a good outlook. One must parlay the outlook into forward motion. Take Stewart, for example. Not only did he have a good outlook about not being promoted the first two rounds, he took action as a result of it.

List all the actions to take as a specific result of the situation, which could not or would not have been realized prior. Many times, although the difficult situation would not have been chosen, it actually frees up mind space to consider ideas, have new experiences or to release other goals or agendas prohibited prior. Need more ideas? Take a look at the items placed on the con list. How can each item be reframed in a positive way? Stewart chose to use the time he would not have had if he was promoted to develop himself and ultimately became more successful as a result.

Now choose three of the most impactful ideas and put them into action!

Attitude in the Moment

When dealing with unexpected situations, which arise without notice and without time to sit and sort out views, it is imperative to keep an open mind and not act on emotion. This is difficult when something is surprising or emotionally jarring. Still, allow time to sort out the ramifications of change, of how something will actually play out rather than reacting to first thoughts or emotions.

When asked what you think, it is almost always okay to respond with something like: "I am not sure, I need to think about it." Being honest is always a good route as long as you do not give up too much of what you are thinking: "I am not sure I agree with the direction but since I have not had time to review what the effects are I am not ready to state an opinion yet." Rather than: "I do not like this, I think it will fail, and I do not want to have any part of it!" You may be feeling the latter, but state the former.

Emotional
Strength

Attitude in Other Areas

Attitude has been reviewed as it relates to disappointment or thrust upon change, but it is also relevant in other arenas.

A store manager at The Home Depot was over his head in the job. Being a store manager was not the right fit for his skill sets or experience. He had not worked his way up in the stores but came from outside the company through a training program. Despite his lack of execution, of understanding, or of pro-active ideas to move the business, he stayed employed as a store manager for over eight years solely because of his attitude. He was open, honest, worked hard, accepted criticism and endeavored to change. His was an amazing story of an attitude that overcame disadvantage. He eventually became a successful store manager. With a different attitude he would have failed in his first few years.

To be clear, the point is to impress how crucial a role attitude plays verses advocating a person stay in a position they are unqualified for. Attitude is a game maker and game changer. One's attitude determines the way others perceive them, how many breaks a person receives, how much help and encouragement; the list is endless. In the store manager's case, it allowed him to maintain a livelihood he would not have had without it while growing into the position.

Outlook

Another aspect of attitude is outlook. Consider the characters in Winnie the Pooh. Tigger always looked at the upside and potential in a given situation with a positive outlook. Eeyore believed nothing would ever work. People tend to want to be around a slightly less energetic Tigger of the world rather than an Eeyore. It becomes wearisome to always have to balance someone else's negative outlook, especially when battling one's own.

> There are some fun personality tests on-line to determine which character you most closely relate to. It can be entertaining and revealing to find out.

Positive Output

Try putting into action the mantra learned in kindergarten with a slight variation:

"If you don't have something *positive* to say, don't say anything at all."

Observe

Watch for situations and monitor your own reactions or get a partner to help if an attitude makeover is needed! *It is important to stress that good constructive feedback done in a healthy constructive way is still positive.*

The What Now Mindset

Another way to approach a setback or disappointment is to ask: What Now? Focusing on the next steps to

8

Emotional Strength: The "What Now "Mindset

reach a desired goal focuses energy as fuel to move beyond obstacles rather than being static.

Success Attitude

Lastly, attitude is just as important when successful, when right, or when winning. Good sportsmanship plays a part in business competition as well. Refrain from flaunting success over others; it may lead to being isolated without supporters. Instead, accept triumphs graciously acknowledging the efforts of others that helped garner the success.

Summary

Having a positive attitude is crucial for success in business. There are many setbacks, disappointments, and challenges to overcome. A good positive attitude, finding the good in each situation, and asking, "What Now?" with action following all, helps keeps momentum going forward.

Chapter Five

Make the Most of Feedback

Receiving Feedback

At some point in life, receiving feedback that is difficult to hear is inevitable. In the workplace this can take the form of reviews, coaching from bosses, a meeting with HR, feedback from a client, or even a formalized feedback session where individuals are asked to answer questions on how they perceive their peers. Although difficult, feedback is crucial to growth and long term success. It is those "Ah Ha" moments, those glimpses from another perspective, that foster needed change and adjustment in order to propel positive growth. Feedback is a gift. Sometimes the giver knows just what is needed and other times they miss. But classifying feedback as a gift rather than an attack allows the receiver to be more open and able to take advantage of and use the information.

Throughout my career I have received many types of feedback including very formal sessions. People from every level I worked with answered very pointed questions on my skillsets and leadership to include my boss, peers, direct reports, and others that interacted with me in some form. Following was a formal session with HR in which we reviewed the results. Feedback of this kind can be a bit stressful, especially if a people pleaser. Other times feedback comes from a simple comment from someone. However the feedback comes in, I tend to look at the very lowest scores or biggest opportunities and focus on those rather than balance them with the areas in which I excel. At first my emotions tend to get wrapped up and take the feedback personally instead of understanding the business aspect of it.

Interesting enough, when I am rating someone else or giving feedback on or to them, I do not view the constructive feedback as an attack on them as a person, but rather a view of their professional attributes. I am optimistic and hopeful that the individual will take the feedback as constructive and make some positive changes to grow as a professional, that I might have a little part in their advancement. I am perfectly prepared to forget any weakness I included in their feedback and celebrate their achievements along with them, as soon as I see a change.

Remind myself about this.

How hard it is when the shoe is on the other foot. The criticism can become demoralizing and confidence stealing. Each time a thorough feedback session is conducted I am brutally reminded that I am still human with all the foibles and weaknesses that come along with being one. I first tend to wave off the positive feedback and become defensive regarding the constructive feedback. I create reasoning and justification why the criticism is incorrect. Then I move to being angry and hurt with a lessoning of confidence. I finally make the move to become more objective and am able to see past the emotion and on to how I can be a better person, manager, and professional. Sometimes the process only takes a few minutes, other times it can be a few days or a week or two depending on how strongly my mind/emotions react. I have come to learn that this process needs to play out and to be patient with myself. Then I can move to a positive constructive place.

Steps to Process and Benefit from Feedback

It is critical to understand that it is completely up to the receiver to determine what will be done with the information. The response will ultimately determine if the experience becomes a positive motivation, discarded without merit, or steals confidence and forward momentum. The receiver is in control of the outcome.

Step One: Take some time and use your emotion

Take some time to digest and process the information. Do not allow first reactions to determine the outcome. Understand that the mind and emotions must go through the change management process and require time to do so.

Make no judgments, and no commitments or changes until there has been sufficient time process the information. It might be as simple as counting to three or ten silently or take deep belly breaths; decide to react later, but pay attention to what your emotions are saying.

These first emotions reveal great insight if captured and used. When first receiving feedback, capture those that garner the strongest emotional reaction: highlight if on paper, create a quick note on a computer, put a star next it, hand write the list on a piece of paper. If it is not possible to make a physical note of some sort, make a mental one.

Then walk away, literally and figuratively, from the feedback and gain some emotional distance. Take enough time to avoid reacting personally to the feedback. Instead view it as a puzzle to figure out, or a problem to solve, or more positively, look forward to see what changes can be implemented to improve from this point. If it is difficult to overcome the personal aspect of the feedback, try to objectively envision the feedback as being given to a character in a play or in a game. Try to understand the intent of the feedback, aside from any emotional response.

Step Two: Sift

Once there has been enough time to process the information, and it can be viewed from a more objective point of view, sift through what was said. It is up to the recipient to implement change. Remember that each piece of feedback is only from one perspective, with one set of experiences and can change depending on the day, the mood, the position, and standing of the person. Sift through what is said with an open mind and a healthy filter.

Organize the data in a way which can be translated into action. Divide the feedback into four categories:

- ✓ Positive

- ✓ Neutral

- ✓ Opportunities

- ✓ Not Applicable - Ignore

If the data is easily manipulated, copy paste into a spreadsheet or other software program where the data can be moved around. Sometimes the data itself will already come in a similar form or use highlighters to draw the distinctions. Or simply create three columns and handwrite as in the example form. If feedback of a similar nature is repeated multiple times, capture that information as well.

Positive Feedback

Once the feedback has been divided, look at the positive and verbally say thank you. It might feel silly but gratitude is a crucial step in moving forward and learning from feedback. Saying quietly is fine, but say it aloud. Thoughts become real when verbalized. This is an important step. Recognize and acknowledge the areas in which you excel. It is easy to jump right to what is perceived as negative without recognizing and acknowledging the positives.

Feedback

Positive	#	Nuetral	#

Opportunities	#	Cat*	Why

*A = Agree   D=Dissappointing   AD = Adamant Denial

Neutral Feedback

Neutral feedback is neither positive nor negative. It neither boosts one up nor shows where opportunities lie in order to help move forward. Beyond reading it, no further action is needed.

Opportunities

Feedback that falls into the Opportunities section is the next focus. It is in this section where the jewels are found; where an individual can move and grow far faster than without them. It is a good idea to thank those that have given feedback. Just softly, verbally say thank you. Observation is a gift given, whether it is accurate or not.

Now, assign each opportunity one of the reactions below:

- ✓ Adamant Denial (AD)

- ✓ Disappointment (D)

- ✓ Puzzling (P)

- ✓ Agree (A)

This can be accomplished by using different color highlighters, capturing on paper/computer in a form, writing a star/triangle/square to denote the difference, or assigning letters as demonstrated. The important point is to differentiate between the four reactions. Next capture why each falls into the first three categories: Adamant Denial, Disappointment, and Puzzling.

A good indicator of an area in need of a closer look is where reactions are the most vehement. The answer to such a strong reaction will give clues as to how to tackle the feedback. Most likely, although not always, those that fall into Adamant Denial are the areas in which there is the most positive growth potential but are relative blind spots. Many times these are the quickest and easiest to fix, although can be the hardest to admit to. The areas where the reaction is disappointment or surprise, but not strong anger or denial, are most likely areas of decent, confident skillsets that are not being recognized. The key here is to make some alterations so the skillsets can be perceived by others. Areas that are puzzling are most likely those that are defined differently between the feedback giver and receiver. Of course, there will be those areas recognized and in complete agreement with. And those areas where no emotional feeling either way exists are most likely not areas needing much dedication to improving.

Step Three: Action

Make a conscious decision on what will be done with the information received. There are three options:

1) Incorporate changes

2) Recognize, appreciate the feedback, and hold for later application

3) Decide it does not apply and move on

For those that fall in the first category, choose no more than three to focus on. Now it is time to create actions for positive forward motion. Follow the guidelines in Chapter 15 – The Secrets of Effective Game Plans. When the first three areas of opportunity have sufficiently begun to progress in the right direction, begin working on more, if needed.

15

Secrets of
Effective
Game Plans

Remember, the receiver decides what to do with any feedback given. Be honest throughout the process. Be open-minded. Refrain from dwelling on perceived criticism, but rather view the feedback as a precious gift and opportunity to see through the eyes of another.

How Feedback Can Change

I had recently been promoted to the Regional Director of Operations and Asset Protection and along with the promotion came more authority over the districts. I thought I had good relationships with the District Managers (DMs), and had received consistent feedback of a very positive nature in my previous positions. A year into the new position I received anonymous feedback from the same DMs. I was shocked to discover how much more critical the feedback had become. I went through the process outlined above, but it took me a couple weeks to come full circle where I could actually benefit from the information. I realized the feedback had become more critical because I affected the DM's directly. In my prior roles I had been a support to them. In my new role I had authority over areas that directly impacted them and their districts.

It is critical to understand that when promotions or position changes occur that have greater direct impact on people, criticism may be greater as well. The higher a person moves up in an organization, the more people are affected. Expectations rise. There are more observers and more judgement. Feedback is going to be tougher. No one really cares about a weakness if it does not affect them, so they may not say anything about it. But once they are affected by it, the feedback will come.

Immediate Feedback

So far the focus has been on receiving feedback with the luxury of time to work through it. This is not always the case. There are times when feedback is unsolicited, unwanted, or during a review where an immediate response is required. There is no time to bring out highlighters and create pages of notes. The process still applies, just in truncated form.

- ✓ Ask for a minute to think about what has been said. Do not be afraid to ask for time to get back to them the next day or the following week to truly consider and bring back actions.

- ✓ Try to look at the issue objectively, which may be hard in the heat of the moment, but see if there is any truth to what is being said. If so, think of what can be done to adjust right away with more thought to come later for a longer term solution.

- ✓ In the case of flat out disagreement, ask clarifying questions to gain understanding as to why they feel the way they do. Ask for specifics for better understanding. The reasons may be surprising and may include miscommunication.

✓ Let the person know if there is still disagreement but be sure to have specific examples illustrating the reasoning.

✓ If they are not disposed to listening, ask them what they would like to be done. If feasible, agree to do it and move on. If not, explain the reasoning. Be careful to be respectful and give factual reasons and not emotional ones. Emotional reasons tend to be biased and result in a loss of credibility.

There are times when feedback is given completely by surprise and it feels more like an attack than a gift. It is crucial in these cases to stay calm and refrain from overreacting.

When I was an administrative assistant in merchandising, the VP's assistant asked to meet with me. She then let me know of three different people that had given her negative feedback regarding interactions with me. One was an individual that looked to me for training and direction, although did not report to me. I was told she felt that I was no longer supporting her and was abrupt and rude in our dealings. The second was a new fellow administrative assistant to whom I was a resource. Evidently she felt I was condescending. The last of the three was the office IT manager who I was told felt his knowledge and position were discounted by me.

I was taken back by this unexpected and unsolicited feedback. I did not agree with it, and thought the feedback to be unfounded and untrue. Inside I was defensive but I was careful not to react except to thank the VP's assistant for letting me know. After leaving the conference room I thought more about the feedback. Although I was angry I gave time for my emotions to ebb and allow for the possibility there might be some validity in the feedback. There was no need to sift and compile as it was all negative. My next action was to meet with each of them to determine the validity of the feedback and what my next steps would be.

After meeting with each I learned that the first two people had misinterpreted my actions. In my effort to transition them into being more self-sufficient, my behavior had been interpreted as rude and condescending. I went from being defensive about the feedback to acknowledging my error. I took the responsibility to explain and work through a transition with them rather than just cutting off their resource. I let them both know my intentions were to make them better and that we would work together to transition them further into their jobs. The IT manager told me he had no issues whatsoever with me and that if he did I could be sure he would come directly to me.

Had I communicated to the VP's assistant what I actually felt and thought up front I would have come across as immature, defensive, and borderline insubordinate. Because I held my tongue and my emotions in check until I could work through it, I was able to learn better communication skills from the situation, fix damaged relationships, and positively alter my behavior towards others going forward. The VP's assistant gave me the gift of feedback and helped me grow.

There is Always a Choice

No matter what the feedback is, or in what form it is delivered, it is up to each recipient to determine what to do with it and how it will affect them. It may be discounted as completely inaccurate or accurate but immaterial. Even with agreement, the feedback may not be incorporated because priorities lie elsewhere. Another person may be having a bad day and lob criticism to divert attention from themselves. Not everything needs to be reacted to. Understand there are times when feedback does not apply and needs no action at all. Other times reaction needs to be immediate. Use feedback to positively motivate, verses demotivating. Go through the steps outlined above, even if just mentally, or tuck it away to deal with later.

Caution: Keep in mind the possible ramifications of discarding feedback. Depending on the source of the feedback, behavior changes may be necessary in order retain a job or be eligible for promotion.

On the other hand, reaction and behavior adjustment because of feedback given can move one positively forward in a way that would have been difficult or unattainable without it. At the end of the day, the choice is yours.

Self-Assessment

List out every strength you have. Then list out every area of weakness or deficiency. Positive attributes are crucial to know in order to balance out weaknesses. Opportunity areas are also crucial to know:

- ✓ So it is not a surprise when receiving constructive feedback and agreement comes easily

- ✓ So areas are already in process of being improved

- ✓ So an open mind meets any ideas others may have to foster growth

Capture Growth Potential

After receiving feedback, write down how each behavior change can help create growth towards desired career or life goals. Try to relate the potential change to a positive outcome. A change in perception will alter how the feedback is viewed and impact the level of openness to implementing actions.

Partner

Partner with a mentor or someone trusted that is not part of the feedback process, especially in cases where it is difficult to determine or accept if the feedback applies. A trusted person may give a different perspective or present information in a more palatable and acceptable way.

Use Anger's Energy

If angry at the feedback, use its energy to help fuel discovery of what to do next. Anger is typically a cover and defense mechanism for being hurt, which means the feedback either hit a vulnerable spot or an area you have put effort into already.

Look for and Solicit Feedback

Receiving and working with feedback is essential for growth. Without it, achieving development goals requires more time. Get in the habit of pro-actively approaching people for feedback. The more often feedback occurs, the less emotional and more actionable it becomes. Instead of dreading and reacting negatively to it, appreciate and use feedback to adjust behaviors in a positive way. In time, receiving feedback can even be looked forward to!

Walk in Another's Shoes

When disagreeing with feedback, try to look at the topic from the other's point of view. Why might they have the perception? What could change the perception?

8

Emotional
Strength

Put on your Emotional Armor

If dealing with emotion becomes a struggle in the workplace, shoring up emotional fortitude is essential.

Have Responses Ready

Having responses ready for situations can greatly help in managing communication and may buy time to utilize the feedback steps. In the absence of a plan, emotion can take over and lead down a road one would rather not travel. Here are some response ideas for unsolicited/surprise feedback.

> "Thank you for the feedback. I need some time to process it."

> "That is a lot to take in at once, I will think on what you have told me and work out how I can adjust."

> "Thank you for taking the time to share with me. Can I get back with you tomorrow or Monday as to how I will apply it?"

Brainstorm

Brainstorm different feedback scenarios and then develop responses to them. Think of prior experiences or the experiences of others and create multiple responses. Watch how others have responded to situations and capture those that were effective.

Practice

Visualize then practice giving a composed response. Having options to choose from can help create a smoother interaction.

Keep a Log

Keep a log of responses either written or electronic. Just the act of writing them down will help to better prepare for the unexpected.

Summary

Getting feedback can be tough. To make it a positive experience it is important not to react emotionally but instead filter through what is useful and can help growth versus what will tear down. For feedback that promotes growth, create actions to incorporate. Let the other destructive feedback go so it cannot fester. When feedback is good there is an accompanying "Ah Ha" that goes along with it or "that makes sense," something that resonates within once the emotional denial, frustration or disappointment is gone.

1. Take some time to process the information. Use emotions as a guide in the proper placing of feedback.
2. Sift through feedback to determine which is constructive and which is destructive.
3. Using the constructive feedback, create a plan of no more than three topics to actively incorporate.
4. Have responses ready for immediate response situations.

Chapter Six

Realistic Estimations

Many people underestimate what it takes to accomplish a project or goal. Invariably the construction is delayed; the research takes longer than anticipated; the cost is higher; there is not enough labor. I find most people create *idealistic* estimations based on the perfect scenario, of all components running smoothly, which rarely occurs in reality. *Realistic* estimations, on the other hand, account for the unexpected, for the roadblocks that will inevitably appear. Realistic estimations build in time and resources in order to create solutions mid-stream.

Typically estimations are made in three areas:

Time, Resources, and Material.

Time

Some of the reasons people underestimate the time it takes to accomplish a goal:

- ✓ Unaware of the actual time it takes to accomplish a task

- ✓ Thinking it *should* take less so assuming it *does* takes less

- ✓ Not anticipating and planning for others' calendars

- ✓ Overestimating the amount of help or resources available

- ✓ Underestimating the amount of help or resources needed

- ✓ Not planning for setbacks

- ✓ Not planning for the unexpected

- ✓ Underestimating the time creativity requires

- ✓ Not taking into consideration rewrites or updates

- ✓ Not taking into consideration others' process requirements

Instead of taking all the above into consideration, typically a best case scenario is created versus a realistic one. If all goes perfect, with no communication issues, no additional projects added, no call-outs, it *might* be possible to complete the project in the timeframe - only if the skill in estimating is truly excellent in the first place. Best case scenarios rarely materialize, so the project is set up for failure. However legitimate the reasons are for the failure, they end up appearing as excuses since the timelines cannot be met and the project not completed. Instead, determine the commitment date based on actual data, and set the project to succeed and possibly exceed expectations. If challenged, the data is available to back up the estimated due date.

This is not a way to sandbag, or always give a cushion in order to not work as hard. It is instead building in and planning for the unexpected in a way that allows commitments to be delivered. This creates a reputation that objectives will be achieved and projects completed on time.

Creating an Estimate

Consider the questions below to help determine how many calendars, resources, and other variables are involved and need to be taken into consideration. Use this data to work through the steps following.

✓ Are there others that must be relied on in order to complete this project?

✓ What other projects/time commitments are occurring simultaneously to this project?

✓ What if another project/task is added to the workload during this timeframe?

✓ Are there time zone issues to consider?

✓ Are outside help or resources required?

Step One: Create an Initial Estimate

<u>Perfect World Estimate</u>

Determine how long the project is estimated to take in a perfect world with no distractions or roadblocks. Make sure to use actual data and not just a feel for it. Do not guess. Instead, do some research to create an estimate based on facts.

In the beginning of March of 2015, I was working with a client who had written a book and was in the process of having it published with a desired date the end of April. At first glance the timeframe appeared to be reasonable. Just to make sure, we took out a calendar and penciled in the action items as we estimated:

1) Find and send to Editor – 3 weeks
2) Rewrites – 2 weeks
3) To Compliance – 2 weeks
4) Rewrites – 1 week
5) Publisher – 5 weeks

The time frame was actually going to take closer to 13 weeks, a little over three months, which meant the more realistic goal for book publishing was June, not the end of April.

<u>Accuracy History</u>

Next, consider the history of accuracy. Does scrambling occur near the deadline because the true time was underestimated? Based on the historical ratio of planned to actual, adjust the estimated time.

A family friend was a curator for a museum, extremely creative and bright, with a high sense of gorgeous detail. She was always working crazy hours the week coming up to a show opening. She had a critical path, an outline of the work that needed to be done along the way, complete with due dates, but always seemed to get behind. As I looked into the detail it was clear she underestimated the true amount of time each task required at an almost three to one ratio – meaning the tasks took almost three times as long as what was listed on the critical path. No wonder she and her crew were working crazy hours to get the show opened on time. She needed to triple her estimates on her critical path. As this was unrealistic by itself, the scope and ideas for future shows needed to be adjusted as well.

Step Two: Calendars/Partner

Look at Your Calendar

Look at your up-to-date calendar to see when you are able to complete your aspects of the project, based on the timeframe above.

I was working with a colleague on a project for Celtic Life & Heritage Foundation, a non-profit public works company out of California. An amazing lady with artistic talent to envy, Joanne was to draw the needed artwork for an educational module and complete by the following mid-week. Looking closely at her calendar, Joanne realized she would be out of town for the weekend, had various appointments in between, and had guests arriving. Joanne only had a sum total of two hours in the five days leading up to the due date in order to complete the artwork — clearly not enough time for a finished product. Alternate plans had to be made.

It is crucial to keep calendars up to date and consider, even plot out, when actual work will be completed. Many times, a close look will alter commitments.

Others

Contact others/third parties who are being relied upon for portions of the project and determine the time frame they will need to complete their aspects of it.

Together with a colleague, I was asked to give feedback on a program that would be rolling out across the nation. A week appeared to be reasonable and I had already checked my calendar so I knew I had the time to review. After attempting to contact my partner in the endeavor, I learned he was out of the country on vacation until the end of the following week. Suddenly a week was an unrealistic timeframe to complete. Had I not checked ahead of time I would have given an unrealistic due date that others were planning around.

Step Three: Build in a Reserve

Assume something will happen that increases the completion time and build in reserve time to allow for it.

When I was the Regional Operations Manager at The Home Depot, my boss needed some information quickly for a call she had and asked if I could get it to her in time. The call was in one hour. When I considered what information she wanted, I or my assistant could easily pull the data in about five minutes. It would take me another five to ten minutes to analyze and about five minutes to put in a format she could use for a total of twenty minutes. Since her call was in an hour I had plenty of reserve time built in and committed to her that I could get her the data prior to her call. When I arrived back at my office, I found my assistant had gone to lunch so she was unable to pull it, which should not have been a problem because I could pull it myself. When I tried my password, it had to be reset by IT and would take about two hours to be updated, and no one else in the office had access to this particular system. Two roadblocks I had to overcome that I was not expecting; it was a good thing I had that extra forty minutes in reserve or I would have missed the deadline. I called a person in another region that had access to the system. They could not pull it right away. It took them about twenty minutes to pull the data and then email it to me and then I still had to analyze it. I was literally walking the data to my boss's office as she dialed on to her call.

You never know what may delay a project. The important aspect is to plan for delays so commitments can still be delivered on time.

Reserve Extension Guidelines

The shorter the amount of time for a project, the higher the increase of reserve time as a percentage is needed. The reverse is also true: the longer amount of time, the lower percentage of increase. Here is a table to start with until accurate ratios applicable to your own industry are determined.

Project Time	Reserve Extension	Example Project Time	Ext Time
Minutes	Triple	20min	60min
Hours	Double	2 hrs	4 hrs
Days	Half Again	4 days	6 days
Weeks	Third Again	3 weeks	4 weeks
Months	Quarter Again	2 months	2.5 months

Step Four: Follow Up on Results

Keep track of actual time per task and a running total for the project. Compare to the original estimate. This helps in future accuracy.

Physical Resources

Just as with time, rarely is the initial estimate on resources accurate. Resources could be monetary, labor, knowledge or any other resource you are dealing with. To start, let's look at money. The upfront cost is rarely ever the end cost. There are many reasons for this, some of them listed below:

- ✓ Needed components were forgotten, overlooked, or unknown at time of estimation

- ✓ Additional scope is added to project

- ✓ Estimate did not include taxes and fees

- ✓ Price increases incurred

- ✓ When actually viewed, quality or assumed application were inaccurate

As a rule of thumb, for projects or purchases less than $50K, I add in an additional 25-33%. I know that sounds crazy, but I have found it to be fairly accurate. Case in point:

Jointly with two other speakers, I was producing a Speaker Showcase in Seattle. It was a small production whose main purpose was to gain updated speaker reel for our media kits. We determined the budget would be approximately $1500 each. Based on my 33% rule I calculated my outflow would be as high as $2000. After a successful showcase I reviewed my cost. With all included, my part of the showcase ended up being

$2103; over the original budget by 40%. In this case, even my additional reserve was not quite enough. A reserve of additional monetary capital is always a good idea. Otherwise the risk is run of either not being able to complete the project at all or causing a different project or need to go unfilled and maybe one that is actually more critical.

$3000 is available to spend on a project.
Known costs add up to $2700, under budget by $300. But the 33% reserve has not yet been added in:

$2700+ $900 (33%) = $3600 or $600 over budget

.

One of three choices :

1) Change the budget - If budget is changed, it needs to be at $3600

2) Change the project

If the project is changed, projected costs should be 25% under original budget, which gives a 33% increase cushion. Here is how the math works out:

25% of $3000 = $750
$3000 - $750 = $2250 initial budget
33% (unexpected costs) of $2250 = $750
$2250 + $750 = $3000 final budget

If using the 25% model the numbers change as follows:

$2700 initial budget + $675 (25%) = $3375 (still over budget by $375)
$3000 final budget − 600 (20%) = $2400 initial
$2400 initial + $600 (25%) = $3000 final budget

3) A combination of both 1 & 2

If the project cannot afford a 25-33% increase in cost, rethink the project whether in scope or feasibility so the known costs are reduced by 20-25% (which gives a 25-33% increase potential).

Budgeting Basics

There are some great resources available to help in budgeting, but here are some quick tips:

Step One: Initial Idea/ Price

Start out with the idea and an approximate cost and compare to what is available to spend. If the cost is not even close with available capital, changes need to be made. Some ideas are: look for ways to get additional capital; alter the project to achieve the same result; revamp the project itself; put the project on hold.

Step Two: Detailed Research

- ✓ List all tasks, actions, and items needed for the project in a single place (simple spreadsheet, for example).

- ✓ Talk with others to help ensure crucial aspects have not been missed.

- ✓ Gather quotes, look up pricing online, do research.   Be sure to add in delivery charges, taxes, fees, the easily overlooked additions.

- ✓ Ensure the tally has a running total and create educated estimates for those expenses lacking precise quotes.

Step Three: Build in the Unexpected

- ✓ Add in either 25%-33% in additional unexpected expenses to the total.

- ✓ To help determine which model to use:

  - 33% Model – when lacking detailed quotes or are new to budgeting

  - 25% model – when possessing very detailed quotes with a lot of experience in budgeting

  - <25% only if an established history of extremely accurate budgeting exists

Step Four: Follow Up on Results

- ✓ Monitor processes and budgets along the way.

- ✓ Keep track of actual resources used alongside the original budget.

Tracking results helps to become more accurate in future budgeting.

Materials

The last area to cover is material both when providing for others or selling, as in manufacturing.

In its simplest form, creating material can be handouts for a meeting. If there are ten people attending the meeting, make a couple extra. Add 10-20% more materials to accommodate the unexpected visitor or a printing issue like a copier error of a blank page.

Step One: Determine Actual Numbers Needed

Do not assume, find out a concrete number.

Step Two: Add 10-20% More

I attended a staff meeting which included the entire regional team and the ten district managers that covered the region. One of the regional managers began his presentation. He only had enough copies for the district managers. Lamely he said, "I only made ten copies, so I guess you will all have to share." His message was not fully received because not everyone could follow along.

I was attending another meeting at Home Depot Headquarters in Atlanta. We were required to bring our laptops and sign into the internet in order to access the information for the presentation. Unfortunately the coordinator of the meeting did not check to ensure there were enough internet plugins in the room (this was prior to Wi-Fi) for all participants. About a third of us could not participate. We ended up switching to a different room and the meeting began an hour late.

Whatever the material being provided, always have more than needed. Check ahead of time and plan for the unexpected.

In its more complicated form, as in wholesale manufacturing, never commit to deliver at full capacity, but instead at 80% of capacity. Expect a machine to break down, for servicing to occur right in the middle of production, for there to be a delay in receiving raw material. One would think this is obvious, but I have seen people overcommit again and again, at very high levels.

In 1999 I was the Hard Surface Flooring Buyer for the Northwest Division. We held product reviews where vendors would bid for the business. I remember a vendor who wanted the business so badly, they committed to deliver product at their capacity and not below it. When the time came to fulfill their order, they had run into mechanical problems at their manufacturing plant and were unable to deliver on their commitments. They were replaced as a vendor, losing a very large account with The Home Depot.

Other Resources

Other resources, like labor, work similar to money. Assume a project will take more labor than initially expected. Using the 25%-33% rule usually works well. With labor unknown variables exist: someone calls out sick, quits in the middle of a project, or the work simply takes longer than expected.

Knowledge is also a finite resource that needs to be taken into account. Does the team have the requisite knowledge to complete the project? If not, how will it be found? How does it change the environment and commitment? What happens if the person with the knowledge quits or is pulled from the project? Make sure to have a contingency plan for the resource of knowledge as part of the commitment. If *you* are the knowledge, what happens if you become sick or are incapacitated in some way with a family emergency or accident? Add in these components when committing to a large project.

Unrealistic Deadlines

There are times when unrealistic deadlines are given. These are almost always negotiable. If the timeframe is not flexible, then usually the resources to accomplish are. The key here is to respond to any pushback with facts and have the decision maker determine what happens next.

I was working as the Executive Assistant to the VP of Human Resources. It was Friday after 6:00pm and everyone else in the department had already left for the weekend. The President of the Division called me and wanted information on the HR policies for UPS that night. I hesitated in answering as the President was very demanding and did not appreciate pushback of any kind. When I did not respond right away, he said, "Is there a problem?"

"Not a problem in getting the information itself," I replied, "it is the timing of it. For the information you need I must speak with the HR department at UPS, which I am more than willing to do. Because it is Friday after 6pm, the people I need to partner with are gone and will not be back until Monday. I am more than happy to pull what information I can online now and send that to you, and then follow up on Monday with the detail you need."

The President responded with a quick "Never mind." and hung up the phone. What he was asking for was unrealistic but I had to show why it was unrealistic. In this case the project was thrown out completely.

Before going on, a quick analysis on the story above is in order. My position was as an Executive Assistant, the one asking for the data was the President of the entire NW Division. Our positions were very far apart. The President was intimidating, a workaholic, and disliked being told the word "No." Yet at the same time, he had asked me for something that was impossible given the timeframe. Some people would have been too scared to push back fearing his response and instead start working on it just to buy some time. In contrast, my response was immediate. Here is the reasoning behind my response:

First, I hesitated because I knew I could not honestly answer in the affirmative since UPS was closed for the night. If I had simply said "Yes" right away, I would have had to call him back and let him know that even though I stated I could do it, I was wrong. Two items of note here:

1) I would have two negatives against me instead of one: first when I gave him an inaccurate answer and then again when I failed to deliver.

2) I would only delay the inevitable answer and possibly upset him more if he had relied on my original answer in his plans. He may have made commitments based on my affirmative and then had to renegotiate or let others know he was unable to fulfill *his* commitment.

It is better to be up front with the truth so all involved can base decisions on facts rather than fear.

Second, when the President asked me if there was a problem, I sidestepped the actual question (since it was more a statement that I needed to comply). Instead, I answered with facts. When I stated there was not a problem, it was stating that I was more than willing to comply and then I continued with the facts of the situation.

Third, I communicated to the President that I was more than willing to gather and complete whatever he needed, gave him options that were possible and then waited for him to determine the direction. I was careful not to inform him of what I would do, but instead presented the facts. This is an important aspect of the conversation so the person in authority makes the decision - effectively giving a new directive.

Lastly, it is important to stay open minded and willing while at the same time being honest with what is possible in a respectful way. Tone and body language are crucial to show willingness to do what is asked, a mindset nimble to adjust to new directives, and emotions balanced so as to move with a sense of urgency with the next directive. When disappointing a person in authority, or making them angry because you are the messenger of news they may not want to hear, it is important to keep personal emotions separate and not take the circumstance as personal.

It can be very scary pushing back against a person of high authority. Being honest in a respectful way, even in the face of fear, can give strength because the position can be backed up with facts. Let the facts be your strength.

Caution
When bringing up a concern like this to ensure work is at a very high level, time is spent efficiently, and arrival to work is on time or early; time is not wasted socializing or taking long breaks. The issue must be legitimate and not the result of being lazy or of subpar performance.

I worked for a Merchandising VP who put an amazing amount of work on me. I was up for the challenge but after working twelve hour days for three weeks straight with no end in sight and still unable to complete all of the work I sat down with my boss and discussed the situation. I showed him all the projects and expectations he had, how much time each of them took and the amount of time I was working. I brought with me five ideas to solve the issue, shown below. In my situation my last resort solution was to hire an additional person that could assist me. My boss was unwilling to change his expectation, but did give me the go ahead to hire an assistant. I continued to work twelve plus hour days until I hired an assistant, but was able to solve the issue long term.

Suggested Solution	Boss's Reaction
Reduce the projects	Not an option
Delay the projects	Not an option
Delegate to others in the office	Not an option
Hire a temp for admin work	No
Hire a permanent PT assistant	Go ahead - 20 hours/week

There are times when the due date is unrealistic, but it is required to buckle down and make it happen anyway. I was working in HR and we had a really big presentation to the President and CEO of the entire company along with the HR VP of the entire company. Two days before the presentation, we received additional requirements of what would be expected. The requirements were completely unrealistic. It did not matter. So I worked, along with others in the department, until 11pm each day and back up at 6am in order to accomplish it. Sometimes, one must buckle down and do what must be done. I would suggest this as a temporary solution. If the job is requiring more than you are willing to give on-going, it is time to look for a new job.

Commitments from Others

On the flip side of giving commitments, it is also important to help those giving you commitments to be realistic and use the same Under Commit philosophy.

When I was the Regional Director of Operations at The Home Depot, I was visiting the receiving department in a store with the Operations Manager. Unfortunately, the department was an absolute mess. There was freight almost a week old in receiving which was causing out of stocks on the sales floor. The manager knew this was not acceptable and was embarrassed at not having looked into it before our walk. I asked when all the freight would be out on the floor and a system in place to ensure execution going forward. She stated it would be done by the following day.

In her zeal to show she had a sense of urgency, and would fix the problem, she set herself up to fail in giving a completely unrealistic commitment.

✓ She missed the very first step in getting an idea of how long the project would take; sorely underestimating the job.

✓ She did not look at the calendar to see what kind of labor she had at her disposal; she was down two freight team associates and one had called out sick.

✓ She did not look at the calendar to determine how many other trucks of product would be coming; four more full trucks were coming in the next two days which would tax her current crew, not to mention trying to catch up.

✓ She did not look at the calendar to see when her Receiving Supervisor worked; he was on vacation for the next week.

And this was only addressing the first step in clearing what was in front of us (all the built up product in receiving). It had not even begun to fix the root cause of broken processes and inadequate staffing.

As I pointed out how she would not be able to accomplish her first deadline, she appeared defeated. Then we began to dig deeper and determine what it would actually take in hours, what resources she would need, and how I could help her get resources. It ended up taking her two weeks to get completely caught up with the help I sent from other stores, and another two weeks after that to bring in and hire the labor that was needed, but she was able to be successful in accomplishing the goal.

When planning around what others are doing ensure their commitments are realistic and can be counted on. If, after gaining others' commitments, they appear to be unrealistic, it is a good idea to add in cushion to your own timelines or resources.

My artist friend Joanne in the first story of the chapter tends to underestimate the time it takes to complete projects because she does not take a realistic look at her calendar before committing. Knowing this, I walk her through the process for a better estimate and then build in extra time in my own critical path so I can still execute the deliverables.

The Up Side of Over Estimating

If able to come in under budget, under time, or under resources... expectations were exceeded! Wonderful! That either means estimates or planning were very accurate or luckily everything was aligned and there were no roadblocks to overcome. It is still a good idea to build in a reserve every time − plan for the unexpected.

Summary

Creating realistic estimations requires research upfront to determine what is needed and planning for the unexpected. It means being able to consistently deliver on commitments. Whether in time, resources, or material, create a reserve that includes the unknown in the commitment equation because, in the real world, environments are rarely perfect, forecasts are rarely exactly on, and life has a way of adding in the spice of roadblocks and challenges that take longer than expected to solve. And if, in fact, all goes well, then expectations are exceeded. Not a bad place to be.

Chapter Seven

Be an Investment

One of the keys to my success was and is the mindset of being an investment versus an expense. We are hired for our ability to grow: grow sales, grow talent, grow ideas; grow in our capacity to contribute. Whether we are hired by someone to join their company or hire ourselves in our own business, we are hired to expand. Without expansion there is no return on investment, whether time or money. Companies do not go into business just to spend money, but instead to get a return on the outlay of time, money, energy, typically in the form of monetary gain.

Early in my career I did not have this outlook. I worked to complete the tasks given to me promptly, checked off the lists my bosses gave me and went home. In my second year with The Home Depot I was promoted to Administrative Assistant and began attending the monthly Stat and Staff meetings where I took notes of the proceedings. More importantly, I learned about the business beyond my small scope. Over the next three years of taking notes I received an amazing education on how the business worked together. Through watching the folly and foibles as well as the consistent successes of the managers, I learned what worked effectively both monetarily and politically. When given the responsibility to co-create the General & Administrative (G&A) budgets for the entire merchandising department, I learned how the Profit & Loss (P&L) Statements worked. Payroll was referred to as both an expense and an investment.

The Payroll line on any given P&L is typically one of the highest dollar individual line items. Some people would say it is one of their largest expenses, but I prefer to consider payroll as an investment, because I expect a return. Invest money and time, and in return receive growth, productivity, and/or profit. If there is no return, then rethink the investment.

Definitions

The definitions of expense and investment are very close, but there is a critical difference. Look at the subtle but hugely impactful distinction:

According to Merriam-Webster.com, the definition of Expense versus Investment:

Expense

- the amount of money that is needed to pay for or buy something

- an amount of money that must be spent especially regularly to pay for something

- something on which money is spent

Investment:

- the outlay of money usually for income or profit

Notice the difference between the two. Expense stops after the purchase. It is basically a trade of money for "things" (either services or product), whereas investment has an expected return. It does not end with the transaction itself but continues beyond. The goal is for the return to not only pay for the resources used to obtain the original investment or ongoing cost to maintain the investment, but continue to return resources beyond the original outlay. In business this is called "ROI": Return on Investment.

Truly understanding the difference can completely change a mindset. These definitions are using money as the resource, but time is also a resource and the same idea can be applied.

I realized I could choose which kind of employee I wanted to be: an expense or an investment. Every person has that choice to make anew each day. I strive to be an investment. It is a mindset differentiator and manifests itself in subtle but significant ways.

Why It Matters

Mindset

A person with an investment mindset relates to the world differently. They strive to find creative solutions, even beyond their job scope. This person tends to look for long term solutions. For example, when in a meeting there are invariably subjects that do not pertain to one's area. So the expense-minded individual tends to tune out during those times, where the investment-minded individual still keeps apprised with what is happening. Maybe their input, ideas, or resources can make the difference in the outcome of a project. Because of the investment-minded individual's attention and impactful suggestion a project could be more successful, going beyond what the individual was originally paid to do. The individual has just stepped over the line from being an expense to an investment.

> **Caution**
> There are companies where no matter how great of an investment an employee is, they do not recognize the impact. Companies that are being acquired, downsizing, getting ready to be sold or going out of business, may shift to a payroll expense view, more of a short term model rather than an investment or long term view. Companies in these phases may begin to lay off good people and cut costs. Determine if the environment supports investment and if not, make a conscious decision: stay or make plans to relocate to another company.

Perception

The perception others have of an investment-minded individual is much higher than an expense-minded person. Investment-minded individuals are seen as team players, as additional resources, a colleague with whom to bounce around ideas. These individuals are talked about when promotions open or for project leaders because of the value they bring to the table. They are able to think beyond the parameters of their basic job and add value to the business as a whole.

Opportunity

More opportunities are created for and by investment-minded individuals. By the very nature of staying engaged and offering resources and suggestions, the investment-minded individual gains exposure to more people in other parts of the business. They learn how other departments work and have a better understanding of how all the different parts of business relate to each other.

How to Do It

So it makes sense and sounds good, now to put it into tangible terms.

Step One: Do the Job Well

The first step is to excel in the current role. If new to a position, starting on a huge project, or are overwhelmed with work, the first step is to learn, manage, then work to create efficiencies within the job in order to excel. This is true for everyone, no matter what position, how high up, or what experiences one has. In order to create a return one must first have a foundation of a job well done.

Step Two: Mindset

The most effective behavior modifier is simply understanding and choosing to be an investment; choosing to add value to the company, department, and position. The mindset of bringing return changes how one interacts with their surroundings.

Step Three: Have a Goal

In 2003 I was promoted to Regional Specialty Manager and I was traveling all over visiting stores in my five state territory. There was very little structure to my role; I could pretty much decide what I did and when I did it. I had sales and productivity goals to meet but beyond that it was pretty much up to me how I structured it. In order to feel that I was doing a good job, that me being there actually made a difference, I had to have a goal. For my purposes, in a for-profit business, my goal was to create a monetary return of three times my salary. I charted out how I might accomplish it. A year or so into my position my new boss, the VP of the region, started having her direct reports do quarterly goals and then updates on accomplishing them. This process solidified my habit of establishing goals and quantifying my return. I could not simply do my job, check off my boxes and then go home. I had to achieve beyond the basics or I would be, however necessary, an expense of the company rather than an investment. Being an expense was not acceptable to me. Investments return, expenses are a necessary evil.

Each quarter, as I created my goals, I looked for areas where I could expand the business, what subtleties I could interject that would reach people in a way to create return. I looked for what follow up or actions I could start that would change the course of sales, reduce an expense, or free up time for the stores.

Step Four: Quantify Effectiveness

I attached an estimated monetary value on each project or implementation I created, or impact I had on others' projects, and then compared it to my salary. I didn't achieve my ideal every year, but there were years where I more than made up for it. For example, when through my actions, different than all the other regions in the company, I added over $1million dollars to the bottom profit by reducing product shrink (the difference in physical product inventory and what is on paper) while other regions were increasing.

Not all efforts are measured in dollars. Effectiveness may be quantified by how many people are helped or trained, by how many hours are reduced by efficiencies or processes streamlined. Maybe effectiveness is measured by managing up well and securing additional resources for the department, being strategic with the resources available and making them stretch further because of processes put in place. Each industry has its own measures. Use what is appropriate for your field.

Step Five: Share Successes

17

Marketing
Yourself

The quickest way to create a return on the investment that is you is to share successes. Others can then take advantage of what has already been proven to work. Many times people try to keep secret how they succeeded in order to remain on top of the rankings, but this is an insecure trait that does not allow the individual to shine or impact areas beyond their scope. Sharing successes is also part of marketing and is imperative for upward mobility. When sharing, be sure to create a specific road map and process guide along with quantified evidence that proves it works. This way the idea or project is readily implemented.

Step Six: Keep Going Back to the Well

Adopting the philosophy of being an investment means continuously looking for opportunities to contribute and make a difference. If one idea does not work or does not pan out, look for another one. If a suggestion is not used do not take it personally, instead keep thinking up new ways to make a difference. Ideally, start with controllable areas. For example, a simple process change to the way a job is done to create efficiencies and allows more to be accomplished for the same amount of time.

Now it is time to start putting these ideas into practice. Here are some suggestions to get started.

Write Goals Down

Create the starting goal. Keep it simple and short. For example, the goal could be: Create one idea each week to contribute to another department in a meeting or strategy session. As with any goals, write them down and set a time to review and note progress. Use a smartphone reminder, create an appointment to review at the end of the week, or create a calendar follow up, anything to help track achievement.

Quantify the Behavior of Others

Notice those that seem to be held in high regard, are team players, always have something of value to add.

What do they do? How do they conduct themselves? In meetings, note those that are engrossed in their world versus those that are attentive. What perception does each give? How does it make you feel about them, how does it change your view of their value at work?

Pick Your Team

If you were given the lead on a cross-functional project and were able to hand-pick your team, within or outside the department, who would you choose? Why? Create a hypothetical cross-functional project to lead. Over the next week create the team solely based on their actions in meetings. How does their behavior in those meetings affect the outcome of your choice? What were the characteristics of those you would choose versus those you would not? How do you incorporate the positive attributes into your own behaviors?

Compile and Track

Create an on-going list of projects and ideas *you* put into motion or positively impacted another's project. Quantify the results either in time, money (increased revenue or decreased expense), people, units or other measurement appropriate to the efforts. Strive to have at least one impactful action each month (or go for something every week, with the goal to achieve at least one per month). Keep a tally and subtotal each quarter. If nothing impactful has been done the previous month, set aside time to think about what can be done going forward. Here is a template to help get you started.

Impactful Implemented Ideas

Unit of Measure: [   ]
Goal: [   ]

Date [   ]   Impact [   ]

Description
[   ]

Date [   ]   Impact [   ]

Description
[   ]

Brainstorm

Create a brainstorming session with peers and/or colleagues on ways to improve the business. Try for at least ten. The first ideas created are usually fairly obvious. The longer the brainstorm session the more creativity is unleashed.

Choose a Success

Go through every success from the past 90 days. Find at least one (try for three) to package and share with others. The implementation can be simple. Focus on the impact not the complexity. The simpler and easier to implement the more likely the idea will be adopted.

 ## Take a Phone Break

Try turning off or silencing smartphones/devices while in a meeting to ward off distractions. This allows for a better ability to stay engaged and offer impactful suggestions or solutions.

Summary

Having an investment mindset creates a higher perception, and more opportunity than for those that do not have the mindset. Of course the first step is doing the job well. Then add value and return.

Step One:	Do the job well
Step Two:	Have the mindset of investment / adding value
Step Three:	Create goals
Step Four:	Quantify successes
Step Five:	Share successes
Step Six:	Repeat

Chapter Eight

Emotional Strength

What is Emotion?

Merriam-Webster.com defines emotion as:

1. *the affective aspect of consciousness : feeling*
2. *a state of feeling*
3. *a conscious mental reaction (as anger or fear) subjectively experienced as strong feeling usually directed toward a specific object and typically accompanied by physiological and behavioral changes in the body*

It is crucial to understand emotions and learn how to use them as a resource. When it comes to emotional strength, having a steady platform to push off from is necessary. Understanding emotions is key; harnessing its energy and power makes a huge difference in success. Women have had the unfortunate stereotype of being emotional, and not the good caring kind but the "can't handle it" type where a bit of "well-meaning" criticism leads to breaking down in uncontrolled sobs. In an effort to combat this notion, women have tried to suppress emotion so much that the opposite stereotype has resulted. Women may be portrayed as ice queens, with no feelings at all. The stereotype is changing, as more women learn and implement the tools not only to create emotional strength, but to harness the power it gives. Let's start with getting a handle on emotions when they burst forth in the psyche.

My emotions are my most stalwart and loyal defenders. Even before my mind has figured it out my emotions will let me know when I have been seemingly or actually attacked, hurt, mistreated, or subverted even when it is extremely subtle. Emotions leap to my defense and are ready for action. I have learned to listen to the warning my emotions give me, heed the knowledge gained, but refrain from taking any action until my mind has time to process. My emotions, although quick to defend, rarely have complete information. Acting on partial information can create misunderstandings, false accusations, deteriorating relationships, loss of credibility, respect and opportunities. Acting on emotion with incomplete facts is like hearing one scout's report and launching a battle, instead of waiting for all the other scouts to make their reports and taking stock of resources, options, and strategy. The information the first scout brings in is crucial but should not be acted upon independently. On the flip side, ignoring what emotion reveals is like going into battle without sending scouts or sending them but ignoring what the scouts report; again, incomplete information and definitely not advantageous.

How to Direct Emotion

Instead of taking what emotions communicate at first feel, allow time to interpret the underlying message: "Be alert, something is happening, action might be needed." Emotions are an early warning system. Heed them and then look, listen, be aware, pay attention, gather more information. There is something going on that is important. It is critical to use emotions as a guide then use the mind to determine what action to take. Using the mind gives opportunity for actions to be backed up by facts rather being swept away by emotion's swift current. Depending on the situation, it is possible to interpret, determine, and take action in a few moments. Other times it may take a few days or even weeks.

While all of the sifting is occurring under the surface, the outward demeanor needs to stay calm and present. Perceived threats kick the body's chemicals into action and adrenaline and cortisol flood the system in preparation of a fight or flight response. Although this works extremely well in primitive surroundings, it is not helpful in the workplace where the typical situation is not life and death. The residual chemicals are not used up with physical exertion (of fighting or fleeing). So while mentally trying to be serene the body, full of adrenaline and cortisol, may betray. The face becomes flushed with all the blood rushing in to give the heart and other muscles the oxygen needed for quick action. Hands shake with the sudden adrenaline rush made for brain and muscles to work at peak levels. Voices may even quiver[1].

The more stressful situations encountered and overcome, the less the body will react with high levels of chemicals in the blood stream. The more confident a person is in handling these situations the less the threat the brain senses and reacts to. The more personal power possessed the less threatening others' actions and words become. But in the moment, when caught unaware, here are some ways to cope with immediate situations:

 Take a walk or do something physical. The chemicals will be used and move out of the body's system much quicker than being sedentary. Even a few minutes can make a huge difference. Use the time to clear the mind of emotion. Take deep calming breaths. The primitive part of the brain will have accomplished its purpose of removing danger. It is good to allow some time to pass before taking any action.

 If a walk is not possible, take deep abdominal breaths. Stress chemicals cause shortness of breath in an effort to bring additional oxygen to the heart. Taking deep belly breaths can be calming.

---

[1] www.youramazingbrain.org/brainchange/stressbrain.htm

Focus all the mental energy suddenly available on what is happening at present, take amazing notes, or memorize what the speaker is saying. Give the mind a purpose until the chemicals can begin to diminish. Focusing on something other than the perceived threat can help the body respond to lessoning the threat level as well.

 It may not be possible to talk or physically participate in the current discussion until emotions are in check, but stay alert and focused on what is happening. Maintain eye contact and open body language to be perceived as still participating even though quiet and inwardly working through emotions. This helps discourage the perceptions of withdrawal or pouting because a decision did not go your way. When maintaining eye contact, make sure to look away from time to time so as not to appear aggressive.

 Use the additional brain power available to figure out possible next steps, even if the steps are simply to walk around the building and get some air. Be cautious of acting on those steps that affect the future right away; sift through fact and emotion first.

 Talk with a trusted friend or colleague who may have a different point of view. Another person may offer clarity and lessen the perceived threat, lessening your stress response at the same time.

Building Emotional Strength

Being pro-active in building emotional strength helps to evade situations that invoke the fight or flight syndrome. Building emotional strength is much like building any kind of strength; it takes practice and application. The more preparation made the more emotional strength will be available when called upon for use. Here are five avenues to create a steady platform of emotional strength.

Job Preparation

One of the biggest avenues to create emotional strength is to be prepared. Excel at work, get educated, read and research to gather facts, prepare for meetings, learn new skills. Those that are truly prepared and know their business are seldom ambushed or surprised by what others may throw at them. In many cases the perception of "attacks" changes. When prepared, challenges come across as debate, as others gathering their own information or as healthy dialogue to vet out possible weaknesses in an idea. When one is not prepared those same challenges can be perceived as ambushes, appear personal in nature, as an attack, and the body responds in kind.

There are times when ambushes occur, where someone *is* trying to attack. Being prepared provides options and the confidence to meet those attacks with facts and backup support. The emotions will still arise because they are doing their job as a warning system and providing adrenaline to sharpen the brain. Now those chemicals can be used as an advantage. Use the energy positively.

 Create a Checklist or To Do list and put all projects on it with a date for completion. Prioritize the most important and complete those first. Refer to the list and mark off when complete.

 Prior to a meeting or call, review all areas of responsibility and ensure all have been completed, researched, analyzed, and compiled. When prepared, one looks forward to sharing and discussing rather than dreading the interaction.

 Be able to back up what you say. When making a statement, have facts and resources to show and lend credibility. Have reports at hand, names of those spoken with, email strings, dates/times/location of conversation or events, quotes. Have the information available, or ability to access it quickly, in case others want to see the resources for themselves.

 Collaborate with others. Getting others' perceptions and ideas helps in recognizing aspects missing in a project, creates buy-in, and produces a higher quality end product that will be more widely accepted.

 Invest in your own development. If an area of the job is a struggle and is inhibiting a job well done, take a class, look for help on-line, ask colleagues or friends who excel in that area how they do it. Take charge of your own development.

The "What Now" Mindset

Whenever I am posed with a setback, whether fair or unfair, I ask myself, "What now?" and then I proceed to answer it. Asking and answering keeps me focused on positive forward motion, not dwelling on the setback itself.

At the end of 2003 it was announced that the Northwest and Western Divisions of Home Depot would be combined into one, effectively eliminating almost all the jobs in the Northwest Office where I worked. It came as quite a shock. The timing could not have been worse. My husband and I had just opened a restaurant and we were still building the clientele. My emotions knew there was action to be taken and pushed all the chemicals in my system in order to react, but there was nothing to fight or run from. Using the "What now?" mindset I instead used the energy to think of options, used the extra brain power to find what opportunities were available and what actions I needed to take – like brush up my resume and start sending out job applications. There was no use dwelling on the past, even though that past was only a minute before.

On a smaller scale I have worked on projects that were not used, or had my ideas shot down by others with no option to appeal. At first it feels like a waste of time, all the work and effort for nothing. After sifting through the emotion it is imperative to learn from the setback using the new information to form the next path, as a guide for the next expedition. For example, if there was something personal in the rejection of an idea or project, what must change going forward to neutralize the personal aspect? If a proposal was not well received, what specific component(s) created the negative response? How can those components or aspects be used, changed, and learned from in order to create a better and well-received project in the future?

Adopt the mindset: Okay, this is the new playing field; I need to adjust. What now? Use the mind to determine next steps with emotion as one piece of the information used. Forge a new path, take a new action. Change the focus, if needed, in order to keep moving. Keeping the mind focused on what is ahead, using information gleaned from what is behind, including emotional reactions to it, actively engages focus in actions that are positive and effective. Use the emotion as fuel to take the next steps and as an indicator of where adjustments are needed. Be willing to let go of the past and move on.

Giving into the setback, whatever form it takes, allows emotion of the perceived failure or unfairness to demoralize and effectively negate influence, value, and success; most importantly self-worth. The idea here is to keep moving forward. If something feels like a personal attack, file the information away for later review and in the moment move forward as if it is not. Emotions will flag what needs to be reviewed. Pay attention, but keep moving.

Emotional Preparedness

If giving a suggestion or an idea to a group or even to an individual, be prepared that it has a 50/50 chance of being accepted. If it is not accepted, ask questions as to why if the reasons have not already been communicated. Understanding the reason behind the decision can help frame future suggestions and give a better understanding of the business as a whole or at the least gives insight to the other person's perspective. At the same time it can remove the sting of the rejection and the possible perception that the decision was personal. Then move on. Focus on the next idea, the next solution or project rather than dwelling on the one not well received.

If a tough conversation is coming up, prepare emotions similar to giving a pep talk:

✓ Go through what the possible outcomes could be

✓ Determine what the options are

✓ Determine possible paths and responses

✓ Get others opinions or ideas if appropriate

In short, prepare and create expectations to avoid being emotionally ambushed. The conversation may still be difficult and there may still be a rush of emotion, but having prepared there is a way to channel the emotion instead of allowing the emotion to be in control.

Honesty

Many people prevaricate when finding themselves in an uncomfortable situation with no out in sight. Sometimes they do not want to disappoint the person confronting them or are afraid of getting into trouble, being fired, or losing face or a promotional opportunity. Whichever the case, people make up what they perceive to be an acceptable answer to get out of the situation. Instead they make the situation even worse because emotions are still whirling around inside and they are running on stress; not to mention the added pressure of having lied and hoping they are not found out, and then trying to fix the issue before anyone does find out. Sure the person may get away with it for a little while, but others see through the deceit and no longer trust what they say. Lying is the antithesis of emotional strength and is used to manipulate or to cover up fear.

Instead, honesty is a much better recourse. When I was an administrative assistant in Merchandising I had the advantage of being a fly on the wall for over two hundred meetings in the course of three years. The buyers (called merchants) reported into my two bosses. Each week or month during the staff meetings the merchants would be asked for status updates on projects. It was very interesting to watch the responses they gave when assignments were not complete. Some would lie and state it was complete and would get to the Divisional Manager later that day. Others would be honest and state the project was not complete but would be complete by a certain date and then would follow up with the action of completion. I found it interesting that our boss would accept the honest miss every time and move on but would ask those that lied for more details and it would become apparent the work had not been completed. I learned early on to own up to my mistakes and quickly rectify. With honesty comes credibility, trust, and a lower emotional response. The miss is already on the table. The next step is to take action quickly and rectify the miss, then work to have as few future misses as possible.

There are situations when a person can be caught off guard with a question where the answer is unknown. Some make the answer up on the spot then have to come back and state they were wrong. The receiving person may have made decisions as a result of the information. Better to delay the answer and be right, then guess and be wrong. Some possible responses instead are:

"I do not know off the top of my head but I will find out..."

"I need to verify my information to ensure an accurate answer..."

"I believe it is _____, but I will verify..."

...and then add in a time frame.

A time frame is crucial. Sometimes the time frame is "right now" and phone calls need to be made, a note sent off, or facts found right then and there. Other times the time frame may be within the next thirty minutes or the next day. If it is a complex answer the time frame may be the end of the week or longer, but always give a follow up date/time. The four components here are:

1) Acknowledge the need to gather information

2) Outline the action(s) to be taken

3) Have a date/time the recipient can expect the response

4) Deliver on the commitment

Emotional strength can take many forms. Honesty is one way of demonstrating it.

Personal Power

There is no better advantage in business and in life than possessing personal power. Personal power is not contingent on a job, the status of a job title, or the working environment. Personal power comes from knowledge, strength of values, and the ability to act on said knowledge and values in the face of adversity. Personal power keeps an individual intact, it is a healthy sense of self, or personal identity. Without personal power identity can get wrapped up in a title, job, another person, or other's perception. This causes emotional weakness rather than strength and can cause people to behave differently or make poor decisions because they are trying to protect their misplaced identity. An element of emotional strength is having the power to change one's environment; to stand up for deeply held beliefs. Here are a few ways to grow personal power.

Healthy Sense of Self

Many driven professionals find their identity and sense of self in their jobs – which can be taken away. It is crucial to find identity in true self, the inner person. No matter what happens in life, true self cannot be taken away, although it can be overlooked and hidden. Investing in true self, discovering your foundational truths and what you stand for, as well as investing in healthy relationships and helping others, is crucial to a healthy sense of self and personal power.

Invest in True Self

Look over the past month. Write down the date and any activity where time was spent investing in the inner-you, your true self, alone. When was the last time you devoted yourself to something enjoyable or fun? Or worked on a personal passion or goal? If nothing comes to mind, this is a good place to start. Carve out time and plan a date for true self, by yourself at least once a month.

Who Are You?

Write down the answer to the question: "Who are you?" that does not include a job description. What do you stand for? What do you value? If you were writing your own eulogy what would you want in it? What do you need to adjust in your life in order for the eulogy to be true?

Invest in Others

Relationships

How healthy are your relationships with other people? Do you give as well as receive from them? List the important relationships in your life. Next to their name include every activity you have done with them over the past month. Look forward to the next month. List all planned time with them. How have you invested in maintaining and improving relationships? If your list is blank, you need to set up time to invest in your relationships.

Giving Back

What have you done to invest and give back to others in need? Do you volunteer or mentor? Do you have a neighbor or friend who you help out? Giving money to organizations is good, but does not qualify for this exercise. If nothing comes to mind, be on the lookout for opportunities. They do not have to take large amounts of time, but helping others is one way to help keep you grounded and balanced.

Identity

If your identity is wrapped up in a title or job, or you lack supportive relationships, consider finding a life coach or a counselor.

Have a Plan B

What happens if the company restructures and through no fault of your own your job is eliminated? What if you are required to do something that violates your morals or belief structure or is actually illegal? What if you are fired? What do you do? It is always good to have a Plan B. One aspect of emotional strength comes from being prepared for the unexpected.

Create an Immediate Plan B, C, D...

Brainstorm alone and/or with friends, family, and others and come up with multiple immediate solutions. Many times other people can see strengths and opportunities that alone are difficult to recognize. This list is immediate so it would not include going back to school for the next four years unless the finances are in place to back it up. This is the "Whoa, what do I do now" list. Use the template I have created or use another form. The important aspect is to create it!

1. Create a list of ten options (or more).

2. List out any roadblocks to achieving each one.

3. What needs to be done in order to overcome each roadblock?

4. Rank each option starting with "B" (this is a Plan B after all, Plan A is your current job).

5. Take action on removing the roadblocks so there is always a plan, just in case.

Immediate Options

Option

Roadblocks	Actions

Create a Long-term Plan B, C, D...

Complete the same exercise but with a longer time frame in mind. Instead of immediate, what if the change came with a year or more notice. What then? Start working towards next steps and plans. To help, read Chapter 15: The Secrets of Effective Game Plans.

15

The Secrets
of Effective
Game Plans

Be Financially Prepared

Having the resources to back up decisions is crucial. Too many people are so afraid to lose their jobs they do whatever it takes to keep it, even violating their own conscience. Those that are not afraid are more effective. They tend to make better suggestions, are willing to take risks and play devil's advocate. They focus on the right decisions for the company and those around them rather than the popular or easy decisions. In order to take risks, one must be comfortable that if something does happen to the job, they have the resources to cover their responsibilities while transitioning to the next job or opportunity.

- ✓ Work towards having 3-6 months of bills in liquid assets to cover a job transition. The higher the bills the more months needed as a safety net.

- ✓ Spend less than you make.

- ✓ Work down debt – change habits to save for what is needed rather than borrowing.

- ✓ Only buy "nice to have's" with cash and not credit.

- ✓ Put away money for savings.

It is amazing how much personal power is created when not living paycheck to paycheck; how many options open up when not overwhelmed with debt, mortgaging the future, whittling down future possibilities. If living paycheck to paycheck start making changes. It may take two to three years to get six months of bills in liquid assets or with aggressive changes it may be accomplished sooner. The important part is to work towards financial goals and have as a safety net.

Track Your Spending

Track where the money goes for the next month or two and look for ways to cut back and set up an emergency fund. Use a software program or app, or simply go through bank/credit card statements and enter in a spreadsheet. The important aspect is to know where money goes so adjustments can be made.

Pay Yourself First

Automatically move money over from checking to savings, just like an automated bill.

Create a Game Plan

Create a goal and game plan on how you will establish and grow an emergency fund. See Chapter 15: The Secrets of Effective Game Plans.

15

The Secrets
of Effective
Game Plans

<u>Get Help</u>

Buy a book on financial planning or hire a financial coach to get on track.

The Power of Emotion

Emotions are highly attuned, but for so long, in an effort to fit in to what society seems to require, many have suppressed or discounted emotions to the point where emotions no longer feed the mind and body critical pieces of information. Since evidence cannot be shown for "hunches," they are ignored. Since instincts cannot be backed up with facts, they are discounted and their valuable message overlooked. Critical to success as human beings is to understand how emotions work. Create a steady and safe platform from which to acknowledge emotion and then incorporate the value they contribute into decisions, relationships, and overall life.

Similar to when emotions leap to defend, hunches are communicating the need to look closer at something or someone. When emotions are allowed to go beyond self and touch others, it is possible to sense when others are feeling uncomfortable, have something to add, or when they disagree. If emotions are shut down, the ability to recognize what is going on around us is lost. It becomes difficult, if not impossible, to discern what is happening below the surface of another. Only allowing for personal opinions or processes means missing out on the amazing ideas and incredible solutions others have to contribute. Use the information emotion provides, those hunches or glimpses of an impression, and ask questions. Draw others out and see what they have to offer.

Summary

It is critical to harness and use emotions as a tool and resource rather than allowing them to run rampant or, worse, and discount them completely.

1) Strive to understand how emotions work and how to use the fight or flight response.
2) Create a steady and safe platform from which to acknowledge emotions by:
   a. being prepared
   b. having a healthy forward thinking mindset
   c. being honest
   d. developing personal power
3) Incorporate emotion's insights into decisions.

Chapter Nine

Cover Your Assets

People sometimes think I am overly and unnecessarily organized when they learn I save every single email and document that I receive or send. They think it a waste of time to organize all files both physical and electronic and, although appreciate my follow up emails, cannot be bothered themselves to reiterate the conclusions or actions as a result of a meeting or phone call.

But these kinds of activities are worth more than the time they take or the storage on a computer. These are the proactive steps I take to ensure clarity of communication and expectation. These are insurances that I have had to draw on many times in order to correct misunderstandings, prove I was following directives from others, or trace what happened in a given situation. A little bit of foresight can not only save a career, but move a career forward.

Communication is Key

I learned this lesson the hard way, almost at the expense of my Home Depot career. Always organized and detail oriented by nature, along with a quick mind, I rarely had to write much down. I felt confident in my verbal skills, trusting that others understood my directives. I was working in the HR department as an analyst. My boss, the HR Vice President of the Division, asked me to go over a project with three other peer managers in the department. I was scheduled to go on vacation for a four-day weekend, so met with them Wednesday afternoon. I outlined the project, gave them the opportunity to ask any clarifying questions, ensured they understood the result must be completed by Friday, and left the office for vacation.

After a wonderful vacation I returned to the office on Monday morning and was greeted by a colleague who said in a worried undertone, "Anne, have you talked with the VP yet?" "No," I responded, "I just arrived." "It's bad, the project did not turn out, and they're saying it's all your fault, that you did not give them the correct directions. The VP is *not* happy."

Armed with this warning, I went to my office, met with the other managers to see what they had done and found they had not followed what I told them to do, but instead created a huge ruckus of additional, unnecessary work with the unfortunate result of not completing the project, nor getting the VP what he needed.

I was called into the VP's office, expecting him to understand they had not followed the direction I had given them during my absence. Instead I was on the receiving end of a tirade in which I played the prominent part of failure. I tried to explain that they had not followed my direction, but when asked if I had sent them any documentation, or written direction, I had no proof to back up my claims as the conversation was mostly verbal with a few jotted down notes that of course no one had. As the VP continued his assault, I realized he had changed his mind as to what the outcome of the project needed to be. Not only had the managers not followed my direction the previous week, but he had a different recollection of what he wanted than I had. I was in a no-win situation. With the tone of bringing a recalcitrant child to task, he ordered me to reiterate what I had done wrong, how I would fix the issue at hand, how I would change going forward, and what I had learned from the situation.

I was angry at being misrepresented, for taking the blame for others' lack of execution when I was not even in the office to make corrections. I was then verbally assaulted by my boss with little respect to my person or reputation. My first response was to match his aggression, using choice words as I did so. Fortunately, for me, the cooler and less emotional side of my brain prevailed. Instead I thought very quickly what could be said, what I really would do differently, so I could get out of the office as quickly as possible. I could then decide what my next steps would be with a clearer head.

Making the
Most of
Feedback

Emotional
Strength

I am sure the VP was very aware of my anger and attitude as I answered with almost clenched teeth and unwavering eye contact, "I should have clarified in writing exactly what you wanted to ensure I understood and received your approval and then put the direction in writing so there was no confusion for the other managers. I will personally do the project so it is done to your satisfaction and going forward I will always reiterate in writing what you have requested enabling you to review and ensure I have the proper understanding before I proceed." I am not pleased to say I had a bit of an attitude and my statement was more of a threat that I would have a record of everything I was asked to do than a sincerely learned lesson, but he was appeased and I left the office.

I look back now and realize that I truly did make a mistake and the fault was at my feet. I genuinely did learn from the situation, all the outcomes the VP was trying to get me to see albeit in a less than respectful leadership style. I changed my outlook and actions immediately. And it has served me well to this day.

Going forward, I followed up with an email to ensure I was on the same page as my VP and waited his response before starting the project. I continued this with others if I felt there was any possibility of confusion. I saved every single email from that point onward, organizing in a way I could quickly retrieve if needed. I cannot even count the number of times I have had to refer to an old email showing the direction given. When others would say I never communicated to them, out came the original email I would then forward to them. With these emails I could show my boss I had completed my part of the business, show notes taken from calls or meetings and sent out, proving that the topic had been covered. Email strings are a crucial part of ensuring assets are covered.

Clarify in Writing

If there is any concern of confusion, type up a synapsis of the project or direction to include:

- ✓ Scope

- ✓ Action Items

- ✓ Assignees of actions

- ✓ Due dates

Request a confirmation from the boss or the project owner that the understanding of the request is correct. Communication is critical to avoid misunderstandings or change of scope.

Partner Ahead of Time

Partnering ahead of time is an excellent way not only to ensure decisions will be backed up, but also to get buy-in, see what concerns others may have that can be pro-actively adjusted, and achieve a better plan all the way around.

When I was first promoted to Regional Specialty Manager, I was charged with overseeing all processes related to specialty (kitchen cabinets, flooring, millworks). In my zeal to make things happen I began various rollouts that Home Depot's corporate office in Atlanta suggested for the region. Some of the local district managers (DM's) did not agree with the changes and went above my head to the Vice President who then called me in to her office and challenged my direction. She did not agree with all the changes and sided with the DM's. I learned to partner ahead of time with a few DM's and run it by them to see what concerns they had, then partner with my VP to ensure all of her concerns were addressed and only afterwards announce the direction. Partnering ahead of time gave me the opportunity to explain the thought process and the advantages, and create solutions to any concerns. Sometimes, it was the better decision not to move forward with the project at all because of concerns raised and lack of support.

Consequently, when I rolled out future projects or direction and there was push back from some in the field, I already had buy-in from their peers as well as the Vice President because I met with them, discussed the project, and made adjustments. Others championed the goal with me and supported the direction rather than challenging it.

Try It

Here is a template to get started which details the information to have ready when presenting an idea.

Idea Presentation

Project Title	
Source of Change/Idea	
Scope	
Reasoning	
Expected Return on Investment	
Needed Resources	
Rollout Timing	
Communication Strategy	
Partnered With/Plan	
Other	

Partnering with Colleagues

It is also critical to gain partnership with those colleagues that overlap with a project or rollout, prior to going live. Business is not conducted in a vacuum and has overlapping effects with multiple areas of the business.

Partnering ahead of time takes more time in the beginning, but it moves a project along faster in the long run because the hurdles have already been dealt with and others already support the idea. Other departments may have unknown requirements or resources. Because I partnered ahead of time, I could confidently make announcements, roll out new processes, knowing I already had the support and backing of the people affected outside my area. I had addressed their concerns ahead of time.

Consider All Departments

Before rolling out the next project or idea, consider all departments or areas of the business it affects. Make sure they know ahead of time by dropping them an email explaining. It is a good idea to send an email even if there has been a verbal conversation. That way they have the details of how it affects them for reference and there is proof of the communication for future use if needed. Use the template below to help keep organized or simply jot down on a paper or computer. The important aspect is to make sure to partner or inform ahead of time. When communicating here are some areas to consider incorporating:

- ✓ What is happening, the scope of project?

- ✓ How does it affect them/their area?

- ✓ How does it benefit them?

- ✓ What is the timing of communication/effective date/etc.?

- ✓ What is needed from them?

- ✓ Address any concerns prior to announcement or the rollout going into effect.

- ✓ What is the best type of communication based on the extent of the effect? A face to face meeting, quick call, presentation, simple email?

Partnering w/ Colleagues	
Project	
Affected Department	
How	Action from them? ❏ Yes ❏ No
Contact	❏ email ❏ meeting ❏ call ❏ other
Communication Notes	
Concerns	

Documentation

Follow Up

After every phone call or meeting where the content might need to be referred to, send a thank you email for their time. Refer to the call or meeting and include the topic covered along with any actions or communication that came out of it. Not only are assets covered, but the note can help others follow through with their commitments as well. Here is an actual email (with a couple slight adjustments in names and length) I wrote to two colleagues after a conference call.

From: Anne Tipper
Sent: Wednesday, May 27, 2015 10:38 AM
To: 'Cindy'; 'Julie'
Subject: Notes from our Call Today

_____

Hello Ladies,
Thank you for the call today to review our status for the speaker showcase.

For your reference, here are the notes / To Do's we agreed upon to complete by this Friday:

    1) Quote & paperwork from Videographer (Cindy)
    2) Dimensions for Staging (Cindy) / Ordering staging (Anne)
    3) Moderator Script: needed from Cindy and Julie
        a. Send Anne short Intros & Topic Titles
        b. Anne will update and meet w/ Marcie on Friday
    4) Venue Contract – Cindy to send to Anne/Julie

Thank you! Have a great rest of your week, and we will touch base next Wednesday.

Anne Tipper

TANGIBLE TOOLS
for women in the workplace
TangibleTools.com

Archive Emails

Saving every single email received and sent is a great way to keep communication and information that may be needed as a reference later. Create an archive folder on your computer. Moving emails to archive keeps them separate from those emails being actively used. When I received about 1,000 emails a week, I kept it very simple. At the end of my work week, I moved all of my deleted items to an archive by calendar quarter. It was easy for me to go back through even 13,000 emails using the search function. For some that is not enough detail. Here are a few possible ways to organize for easy reference later.

Create an archive by:

- ✓ Year
  - ○ Create folders within by quarter for received emails.
  - ○ Create a separate folder for sent emails.
- ✓ Category
  - ○ Organize the type of emails received into no more than five folders.
  - ○ Create subcategories under those five if needed.
- ✓ Project
- ✓ Sender type - A friend of mine organizes by family/friends, vendors, suppliers, clients, and so forth.

Whichever way of archiving is decided make sure it is maintainable. I tried to organize by clients or project, but was unable to keep it up week after week so opted for a much simpler style. Understand the more complicated the process, the harder it will be to maintain. At the very least, once a week move all inactive emails, regardless of content, to a folder for that calendar quarter. It only takes a few minutes.

Keep a Log

Keep a log of those conversations or meeting notes that are not already in emails or another form. Include copies of agendas, notes, and any other important pieces of information. Electronic copies are a great way to keep these so as not to have hundreds of physical files. Electronic files can also be easily accessed remotely. Just make sure to have a good file management system for easy reference. A manual log can also be used. I had a colleague who carried a journal everywhere she went and kept all her notes from every meeting, call, and conversation she had. She dated each page and could refer back to what had occurred in every setting.

Back Up Files

Consistently back up electronic files in case of a computer failure, internet outage, or other unforeseen occurrence. Ideally set up an automatic back up daily, but if this is not possible then weekly, bi-weekly, or at the least, monthly. If automatic back-ups are not possible, make sure to set up a reminder to manually back up all files to a separate source other than your computer. Investing in an external hard drive can be a career saver.

Summary

Covering your assets can take on different forms. Start with great communication and partnering from the beginning, to avoid situations where there is a need for protection. Save documentation such as email strings or follow up notes from meetings. Covering your assets is a form of insurance that will invariably be needed to refer to for proof of work or performance, or in order to steer clear of misunderstandings. Creating a simple archive and follow up process is crucial so it can be maintained.

SECTION TWO

In the Limelight

Chapter Ten

Listen with Intent

Gaining Information

Applied information and knowledge is power. It gives the possessor the ability to create and take advantage of opportunities. It can be a truth serum. It can be the difference between keeping and losing a client. It can be the difference between impressing a boss and failing to meet expectations.

Gaining information to do a job seems obvious, but many people dismiss its importance and miss opportunities to excel. Instead people listen silently, sometimes distractedly, to the directives given and then execute what they *think* is wanted missing the bar the leader set forth. On the flip side, the leader may not give all the information needed to fully complete a task or project to their level of expectation. The leader may assume others understand what they are talking about, may not communicate effectively, or may have just forgotten to include a salient point. When a leader does not communicate fully or the recipient does not listen well, one of two things happen:

1. The receiving party fills in the gaps the best they can and hopes or assumes it is correct.

    OR

2. The receiving party asks clarifying questions to ensure understanding of what is expected, in order to successfully complete the objective.

The result of option one usually ends in the objective not being completed to the satisfaction of the leader (or client). Then the leader faults the distracted listener for not following the instructions.

Clients
This same scenario applies to clients. Clarifying questions are an essential part of communication and integral to the success of meeting a client's expectations.

Early in my career, when I was the administrative assistant to the Vice President of Merchandising, I attended most meetings with my boss and took notes. My boss travelled extensively so was rarely available for follow up questions later. Many of the managers in the meetings would listen but not ask any questions. After the meeting was over they would come to me for clarification. My boss tasked me with ensuring everyone completed their projects. This proved difficult if I could not answer questions they had regarding expectations. As a result, I listened with the intent of gaining information in a different way than if I was only taking notes.

I had to gain the information needed to actually carry out the directives. I had become a resource for all the managers that reported to my boss. My boss would even direct them to me for clarification. I approached every subject as if I would be responsible in some way, never knowing to what extent ahead of time. In the midst of a meeting, where every person there was in a higher position than me, I still had to gain the critical information needed to accomplish the tasks that might later require my involvement. That meant listening with intent.

Types of Intent

Executing / Rolling Out

Listen with the intent and expectation as the person responsible for executing or rolling out the project/idea. It may not happen, the project may be executed by those intended, but having the information in case accomplishes several objectives:

> If Executing the Objective: If there are any concerns of misunderstanding or the leader has a reputation for changing the scope without communicating, make sure to write down your understanding and send to the leader for confirmation.

9

Cover Your
Assets

✓ Better understanding of what is happening beyond one area of responsibility and how each part fits in the whole and inter-relates

✓ Advantages in future meetings, understanding the difficulties and challenges other areas are faced with

✓ More business savvy when it comes to asking for and receiving needed or wanted resources

✓ The ability to step in during a colleague's absence

✓ The ability to offer ideas and solutions, and possibly resources

✓ Receiving stretch assignments showing versatility and capabilities that otherwise would not have been given

✓ Others see your capabilities beyond your current role

If after listening to everything that is stated there is crucial information still outstanding, ask clarifying questions to either get the information at the meeting or find out where the information can be found.

Teaching or Training

Listen with the intent that teaching or training another will be required. I cannot count the number of times I have been asked to teach or train someone that missed a meeting, training class, or conference call. Knowing that I might have to train another changes the way I listen. I listen much more intently, take copious notes, and ensure I understand every facet. I know I may be the one standing up at the front of the room or with another one-on-one to ensure understanding. If the teacher or trainer does not impart all needed information, it can come back on them when the recipient misses something later on.

A colleague of mine was to teach a leadership class to a group of department supervisors. The afternoon before the class she had to cancel and asked if I would teach the class for her since I had been at the same training she had. Because I listened intently to the class originally, I was able to step in and train the class.

Even if not called upon to do so, listening with the intent of training another ensures a more thorough understanding of the subject. This approach can also enable the entire group to have a better understanding simply because of the questions asked while listening with intent.

Defending

Listen with the intent of having to explain or defend. I had just been promoted to Regional Specialty Manager and I flew back to the headquarters in Atlanta, Georgia for my first meeting with the Specialty group. It was a small gathering, just five of us from the field and two or three managers from the corporate office. I was so excited that a new routine was being introduced so that I would have something to kick off my new position. I listened intently, asked every question I could think of regarding the process and felt armed and ready to roll out it out to my sixty-five store region.

My first meeting was with the Seattle district comprised of twelve stores. I very clearly laid out the new program, how it would work, and what the specialty managers needed to do. At the end of my presentation one of the managers asked me why we were changing to this new process. It was a simple enough and valid question, but I was completely dumbstruck. I had no idea why. I had been so excited to bring something new I had not even considered the business reason. In my deer-in-the-headlight moment, my mind scrambling as fast as I could, I knew I would never allow myself to be in that position again. The manager asking the question took pity on me and said "Never mind, we can follow up later" and I closed my portion of the meeting.

From then on I always made sure to find out the reasoning behind the idea, the purpose for the decision, the goal that was trying to be achieved with the change. In short... the why. Understanding why helps in asking better questions, raising relevant and more effective concerns, and gives the entire picture of the process.

Many times the answer as to why a process is changing, or project is being rolled out, will be covered in the information whether vocally or in print. Be on the lookout for it. If not, ask questions in order to gain an understanding of the bigger picture.

Information Checklist

Who

- [ ] Who is leading?
- [ ] What departments are involved?
- [ ] What is my responsibility?
- [ ] Who is involved in my department or team?
- [ ] Who is affected?
- [ ] How will it effect employees/the business/clients?

What

- [ ] What is the project?
- [ ] What are the expectations?
- [ ] What are the parameters?
- [ ] What is the priority?
- [ ] What does the transition look like?
- [ ] Is there any down time as a result?

Where

- [ ] Where is it happening/effecting?
- [ ] Where does it effect?
- [ ] Where are the meetings/follow up?
- [ ] Where does training take place?

When

- [ ] What is the timeframe of the project?
- [ ] When does it start/go live/transition?
- [ ] When will it be finished?
- [ ] When does training take place?

How

- [ ] What is the process for accomplishing?
- [ ] What is the structure for accomplishing?
- [ ] What resources are provided?
- [ ] What resources must I/we/they provide?
- [ ] How much time and resources will this take?
- [ ] What is the budget?
- [ ] Are there checkin meetings/communication?
- [ ] What is the form/cadence of communication?

Why

- [ ] Why are we doing it?
- [ ] What do we hope to gain/achieve?
- [ ] What is the goal?
- [ ] What are the downsides?
- [ ] Why now?
- [ ] How does it fit into the overall business plan?
- [ ] How does this get us closer to our goals/vision?

Which Questions?

When gathering information it is good to start out with the Five W's +How. The template previous is a start on the kinds of information to be listening, looking, and asking for. Add in additional questions as the list is used.

Approach

Stay Focused

The first approach to gaining information is to listen. Pay attention to what is being said. Refrain from chitchatting with others, reading emails, or texting during a presentation. Otherwise, pertinent information may be missed inhibiting the ability to ask questions appropriately. Nothing states more clearly lack of attention and lack of respect than asking a question that was already covered. I know this appears obvious, but I have seen people at very high levels engage in distracting conversation hampering the smooth execution of the very project being reviewed, not to mention showing a blatant disrespect for the presenter. Focus on the topic at hand, truly being present and engaged.

Read the Material

If there are handouts, links, or material accompanying the information, read through the documentation. Keep in mind the information checklist of questions (from the previous form) as the material is reviewed and look for the answers.

Write down any questions and then give the presenter (whether on a call, one-on-one, or meeting) the chance to cover the information. A little patience can go a long way. Interrupting questions about material which will be covered demonstrates impatience and can interrupt the flow of the presentation.

Ask Questions

If the information is not relayed then ask questions. As a general rule, I ask questions when the leader or presenter of the project is there. When I have waited to connect with the person after the meeting or on a follow up call, many times I have not been able to touch base with them in a timely manner. It is better to gain everything needed while with the presenter and saves them time as well. This usually means asking during the meeting or presentation or during the Q&A at the end. Depending on the environment, questions may be asked of the presenter directly after the meeting is over. Trying to get additional information at a later time can become more difficult as each person moves on to other priorities on their plate.

Couching

All questions are not created equal when trying to gain additional information. Couching, along with the correct tone, is important. A direct question may not be as effective politically as an opportunity question. For example:

"What is the communication cadence?"

Depending on the tone used, this question may be perfectly fine or may come across assuming the presenter did not come prepared with the answer missing a critical piece of information. It may put them on the spot and create defensiveness. Another way to phrase the same questions is:

"Is the communication cadence covered in the material?"

Phrasing the question in this manner gives the presenter the opportunity to either shine because the answer is yes, or they can answer it right there. If they do not have the answer they can communicate how and when the questions will be answered. This gives the presenter an out in case they did not prepare or a gracious way for them to remember to discuss it. Try to frame questions as you would want to receive them, both in tone and phrasing. Make sure to agree on how and when information will be received if not already conveyed in the answer. Otherwise, it is easy to lose track and not receive the information.

Tone

Tone is very important and hard to communicate in written form. Meaning changes drastically when tone differs.

<u>Practice</u>

Practice saying the first sentence ("What is the communication cadence?") in different tones and ask others what meaning they hear. Try to communicate each of the tones listed in the table below. It is critical to use the correct tone in order to be effective.

Now try saying the second sentence using different tones ("Is the communication cadence covered in the material?") and see how the meaning can be altered.

Supportive	Serious	Exaggerated
Happy	Conciliatory	Sacchrin
Genuine	Rude	Bitter
Hesitant	Comical	Aggressive
Unsure	Sarcastic	Antagonistic
Confident	Condescending	Resentful
Direct	Patronizing	Gloomy
Exacerbated	Mocking	Bored

Appreciate

As simple as it sounds, remember to say excuse me, please, and thank you. It goes a long way. Continue to use good manners in email and other interactions. Proper behavior in a meeting may be seen as a show if not consistent with other communication.

When Asking During a Presentation Is Not an Option

There are times when one must gather information after the fact. In this case I suggest putting all questions together and seeking answers at one time. People will get impatient with multiple requests. It makes the sender appear disorganized. I prefer emails because there is a written trail of questions and a direct response, but setting up a call can create rapport with the individual, which is fantastic.

Once the answers have been received it is usually a good idea to share with others that were at the same meeting and with the boss. This ensures all are aware of the updated information, prevents double or triple work, and gives credit for knowing what needed to be clarified or gained, gathering the information, and sharing with the team.

When Not to Ask

Sometimes it is inappropriate to ask questions in a public setting. Determine what is applicable specifically for the situation. Here are times when not to ask:

- ✓ the question would come across as an attack or as antagonistic

- ✓ it is clear the presenter does not know the answer

- ✓ there are ulterior motives or an attempt to manipulate the situation

- ✓ the presenter has already said to hold questions for the end

- ✓ others are raising their hands: if having personally asked quite a few questions give others the chance

- ✓ too many questions have been asked already and have become a distraction

- ✓ asking disrupts the flow

- ✓ there is limited time

- ✓ the environment is not conducive

- ✓ the questions are counterproductive

I was in a training class for a new mobile ordering system. I really wanted to learn the information and the Buyers in the class needed to know how to use the system when they were visiting the stores. I noticed most of the Buyers were listening but not with the intent to really learn it, as no one was asking questions. I could tell most of them did not understand the information. So I started asking questions for them. Instead of this helping all I did was irritate the trainer and disrupt the flow of the class. Once I realized that I posed more of a hindrance than a help, I stopped asking questions and set up time with the trainer after the class to learn more of the system.

Another time I was in a meeting where the presenter clearly was not prepared. He had stepped in last minute to cover for another colleague who was out sick. A senior manager in the audience, I will call Tony, disliked the presenter and decided to take advantage of the situation by peppering him with questions it was obvious he did not know. Tony was badgering the presenter. Instead of Tony proving his point that the presenter was unprepared (which we all knew already), he instead proved that he himself was a jerk, and showcased his own lack of professionalism. If you don't care for the person presenting, check your motives and tone to ensure you come across professional and appropriate to the setting. In this case, Tony should have refrained from asking questions.

Some Quick Do's & Don'ts

Do...	Don't...
Pay Attention	Chit chat with others during a meeting
Participate	Simply absorb and observe (unless that is your role)
Read through the material and take good notes	Figure there will be time later to review the material and commit to memory later
Ask questions when it appears the answers will not be covered	Be silent hoping someone else will ask the question
Share with others information you find out	Quietly gather information without sharing
	Assume information will be given that has not been covered
	Wait until later to find answers when the expert is available now

Summary

Information is needed in order to perform, excel, and be successful in the job.

Listen with the intent of

- ✓ Teaching or training others
- ✓ Executing or rolling out
- ✓ Defending the project or rollout

Pay Attention

- ✓ To the presentation
- ✓ To the material laid out

Gain Missing Information

- ✓ Through questions
- ✓ Through follow up
- ✓ In a respectful way mindful of tone

Chapter Eleven

How to Raise Concerns

While raising concerns is crucial, it is only the first step in a series. How concerns are raised makes a huge difference in its reception. Starting with a scenario, what do you do in the majority of situations?

When Do You Raise Concerns?

You are in a meeting with about ten others where a new initiative is being presented. You have some concerns about the project. You:

a. Wait to see if someone else brings it up

b. Discuss with the peer sitting next to you at a break

c. Voice your concerns in the meeting

d. Speak with the presenter after the meeting to let her know your concerns

Each option can be appropriate depending on the situation. That being said, about 80% of the time, I choose option:

c. Voice your concerns in the meeting

There are many advantages of voicing valid, universal concerns during a meeting or conversation versus waiting until later: the meeting or conversation is more time efficient; clarity creates fewer mistakes or delays later; highlights areas that may have been missed; everyone present is able to hear the answer; can give a springboard for assignments outside normal job duties; gives exposure to people in other areas of business.

When choosing option C, first be sure concerns are valid and have a material impact on the project or process. If the concern is petty let the concern go. Second, the concern must be universal. It needs to effect more than one individual. Third, timing is critical. Wait until the presenter has finished the topic before interjecting.

Here are the other options and when it might be a good idea to utilize each.

a. Wait to see if someone else brings it up

If always the first one to raise concerns, sit back a little and give others the opportunity to shine. Others will have a different perspective and only raising your concerns leaves little room for others to contribute. Without a skilled facilitator, many times the most vocal person in the room will shape how the discussion moves. Allowing room for others to bring up their own ideas may give a more well-rounded outcome.

b. Discuss with the peer sitting next to you at a break

This is a great tactic in case something was missed, to get another opinion before raising a concern, or to clarify. After the brief discussion if the concern is still valid, and it is not petty, then raise it. Be careful not to distract.

d. Speak with the presenter after the meeting to let her know your concerns

This is a great avenue to use when the concern is not universal meaning it only effects one area. It is good to use if bringing up the concern publicly would come across as an attack on the presenter or be in bad form politically. It can also be used when the concern, although valid, highlights a mistake the presenter or their team made, for example, bringing up a typo in a technical manual. It may need to be communicated but there is no reason to bring it up publicly.

Be Ready to Suggest a Solution

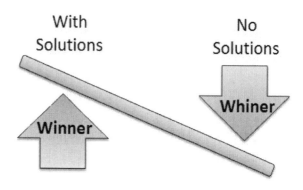

12

Be a Solver

If a person only brings up concerns with nothing to follow it up with, the person can be viewed as a whiner. When concerns are brought up accompanied by possible solutions perception changes. People are more receptive if not faced with trying to solve everything on their own. Solution-based concerns make the project better and solve potential issues before being manifested in a real environment.

The other side of bringing up concerns is that the individual is often times asked to create the solution to go along with it. As a leader I have used this tactic many times. Sometimes it is the leader's way of weeding out whiners and irritants. Sometimes the leader does not have a solution or have the time to create one. A motivated person can have an opportunity to shine.

Before Making a Suggestion/Solution

Ask these three questions before piping up and making a solution suggestion:

1) Does it align with the vision of the company?

No matter how amazing the solution might be, if it does not align with the company's vision or the leader's vision, it will not be met with success. On top of that, the person presenting the solution appears to be out of touch with what is happening.

2) Are there sufficient resources to implement?

The idea could be absolutely fantastic, but if it is unrealistic then it is a waste of time. The idea person is showing they are not in touch with reality, with the constraints of the company; they are not thinking with the whole business in mind or are showing their ignorance. Better not to voice the idea than have the perception of not understanding how the whole works together.

3) Would you, if capable, implement the solution yourself?

As discussed earlier, many times the person bringing up the concerns also gets the task of not only coming up with the solutions but of implementing or rolling out as well. It is much easier to think in the proverbial "someone else." Creating a solution you are personally willing to implement will typically lead to a better result and be accepted by others, notwithstanding the fact that you may be called upon to complete yourself. If the solution is technical, where you lack the expertise or resources to accomplish, still use the framework. If capable, would you be willing to execute? You could be given the resources, or be put on the advisory team.

After considering these three questions, if *all* are answered "yes," then carry on. If *any* are answered "no" then rethink and adjust the suggested solution to meet all three parameters, or simply remain silent.

Political Ramifications: Consider if the solution will be perceived as over stepping bounds, taking someone's resources, or causing another to appear inept. If so, the suggestions may create animosity. Before voicing, determine if the suggested solution is worth the possible fallout.

Volunteer Resources

Volunteer to assist with the solution – this is where stretch assignments may be created, where skillsets can be utilized that have not yet been seen by others. Doing so publicly gives you the credit and not someone who steals the idea. Following up a solution with resources is also a great way to show investment in the successful outcome of the concern. Volunteering can be as simple as a follow up email, as complicated as becoming the project manager, or anything in between. It is critical to assess available bandwidth prior to determining the volunteer level. Also, be cognizant of the organization's culture. Some organizations have very strict protocols to work within.

Here are a few examples of volunteering resources.

- ✓ Send a follow up email outlining the solution to the presenter

- ✓ Email others that may have additional ideas on the subject then circle back and give an update to everyone involved

- ✓ Send the leader the contact information of the people that are vested in the outcome

- ✓ Send a list of resources compiled

- ✓ Coordinate a brainstorming meeting or conference call

- ✓ Gather information and send out to the group

- ✓ Create and compile a survey

- ✓ Interview others

- ✓ Delegate to subordinates part of the project or information gathering

- ✓ Set up meetings

- ✓ Create a prototype idea

- ✓ Create a presentation for the group

- ✓ Be the main contact for the project

✓ Execute completely

Depending on the specific field and company, the examples above may or may not be apropos for your industry or environment. The crucial piece here is to volunteer and it can be something very simple. It is more critical to be a part of the actual solution versus the level of participation. Only you can determine what is appropriate. Different solutions call for different amounts of participation.

Approach

Over the years, through trial and error, I constructed a cadence for approaching concerns. This approach is successful whether in a formal meeting, a conference call, or even an informal discussion with only one other person. There are three steps, each with a pause in between, to gain feedback and assess before continuing.

Step One: Question

Raising the concern in the form of a question allows time to determine if it is appropriate to carry on to the next step of stating a suggested solution. It gives the presenter the space to acknowledge the concern and give a solution, explain why it is not a concern, or open the floor to the questioner. The presenter may ask the questioner to discuss after the presentation so as not to lose the flow. The important aspect of couching the concern with a question is that it gives an opening. If the concern is received well and the presenter yields the floor, then move on to Step Two, otherwise there is no need to continue. Keep in mind the culture in the organization or just the feel of the environment may not be conducive to suggestions.

Step Two: State the Suggested Solution

Step two is where the suggested solution is presented. Again, pause after the suggestion has been stated or questioned to wait for their response. For example, the suggestion can be couched as a question: "Have you already thought about...." This form of couching gives the presenter the respect of already having considered the possibility. The kind of feedback received regarding the suggestion will determine the next step. If the suggestion is well received move forward, otherwise stop here.

Step Three: Volunteer Resources

Quickly follow up with volunteer resources. Ideally, bring them up before being asked. If the resources are not needed, the presenter will say no.

Summary

Raising concerns is an essential part of success. However, it cannot stand alone. The solution's creator ideally has:

1) the ability to recognize and raise valid concerns
2) the where withal to create solutions
3) the understanding at what level to volunteer their own resources in pursuit of a successful outcome

Concerns must be met with solutions that keep in mind:

1) the company's vision
2) the company's resources
3) the individual's willingness to implement said solution

Chapter Twelve

Be a Solver

A Solver takes an active role in changing the status quo. A reporter lets other people know about the changes with no responsibility themselves except to relay the information accurately. Throughout the course of a career both skills are needed. In order to move up in an organization the balance of the two must be weighted more as a Solver. I learned this lesson the hard way.

The Solver Lesson

I was a Financial Analyst with the majority of my job to analyze data and present in an accessible way to those making decisions. I was an excellent reporter. After a restructure, I was promoted to Regional Specialty Manager, where I oversaw all flooring, décor, kitchen cabinet, and millwork processes for the region which consisted of about sixty Home Depot stores. About a year into the position, the Division President and Finance VP decided to hold quarterly business reviews with each region. The District Managers (DM's), who were over all departments in their ten store district, would present their key metrics to the group. When the DM began to review a portion of the business for which a regional manager had oversight, the two would co-present. That is where I came in.

One aspect of the presentation was to forecast sales numbers compared to the plan or budget set forth to achieve. Being analytical and detail oriented I was very confident in my preparation and knowledge. For several districts I quite clearly pronounced the district would miss their sales plan. I had all the analytics to back it up, I was confident. Then the wind was knocked out of me. I was benched. Literally. Part way through the review, after half the districts had presented, the Vice President of the Region benched me, announcing to the entire room that I would no longer be presenting.

I was humiliated and embarrassed in front of all my peers and the officers in the room. I was angry. I seethed in my chair. I had plenty of time to think since I was not allowed to talk for the remainder of the day. I felt unjustly managed. I thought I was being benched because I was unwilling to lie, to misrepresent the truth, to commit to metrics that were impossible, setting me and the region up for failure.

The meeting was over and I went back to my office. While talking with my husband on the phone venting about the meeting, the VP came into my office. I was asked if I understood why I was not allowed to say anything. I communicated my frustration and anger of what I thought was unjustified retribution. It turned out my VP didn't want me to lie; she wanted me to be a Solver instead of a Reporter. It appeared I was giving up and not taking any action to mitigate the sales loss. She wanted me to make a concerted effort to change the status quo, not accept it; to fight for success, not give in to defeat; to be an active participant in a positive outcome and not just an observer.

It was a hard lesson for me but one I remembered.

The next business review I was ready. Prior to the meeting, specifically in those areas that were running below sales plan, I partnered with the Installed Sales Managers. We brainstormed action plans to increase sales. I partnered with the Store Managers and Specialty Managers in low performing areas to come up with sales drivers and increase staffing and training. For all areas I forecasted out the current run rate for sales, and then determined how much I believed the changes we were making would affect the sales. I updated the sales forecast that, although did not hit budget every time, showed the positive impact our actions were taking.

I began creating solutions, instead of reporting the status quo.

When it was my turn to get up and present, not only was I confident and prepared like in meetings past, but this meeting I showed the actions we were taking to change the issues before us. I was an effective manager, leader, and resource for the entire region.

Manager Definition

All types of managers whether entry level, directors, or officers are expected to create solutions for the issues they find. It may not be written out in the job description, but by definition, a manager is:

> *"a person who has control or direction of an institution, business, etc..."*

> *"a person who controls and manipulates resources and expenditures..."*

dictionary.com

Not all situations are as emotionally impactful and career forming as my experience, nor are as far reaching in terms of consequences. Most are far simpler without the drama. But the same rules apply whether in a board room or a break room. Be the person that can bring forth solutions rather than just announce the facts. Be a Solver.

Four Types of Employees

There are four types of employees, whether managers or subordinates. Each person embodies all four at different times. The question is which is dominant and when to bring each to the forefront.

Whiners

Whiners are people that do the tasks required of them, and for their extra gift to the company, inform their boss, peers, or anyone that will listen to them, of all the things that the company should do better. They complain about every problem and issue. They state the facts as they see them, not looking beyond the scope of their job, never once thinking they should get involved in the solution itself. After all, they are already doing extra by bringing up concerns that someone else in a higher pay band should fix. These employees wonder why their bosses are not overjoyed to see them, why they are not appreciated. They do not see themselves as complainers and energy drainers and fail to recognize that is exactly how they are perceived.

The future of the Whiner can be bleak, for the Whiner becomes a thorn in the side of the manager. The Whiner may be the first to lose their job in a restructure, or best case will likely be avoided and given information second hand.

Taskers

Taskers watch the news. They rarely do more than the specific expectations expressed. They rarely complain and do not criticize like the Whiners do. Taskers simply punch in and out quietly carrying out directives. This type of employee is surprised when they do not receive praise and recognition for only doing their jobs. They are not at the forefront for new positions, nor recommended for promotions. These are the workers that become resentful when, during their review, are chided for not taking care of things they see out of place. They are incredulous for they were never told to do them; they would have done it if it was asked of them. The Tasker blames the boss for not asking or telling them the expectations – because how were they to know?

The future of a Tasker is to remain stagnant right where they are until there are no other qualified people and only by default does the Tasker move up. Over time they get promoted, but it is a long trek.

Workers

Workers get their jobs done and if they see something minor or simple off kilter they take care of it. For example, this is the person that will see a piece of trash on the ground and throw it away. They will not walk by it like a Tasker will (because, after all, the Tasker was not specifically asked to pick it up), they will not complain about it like a Whiner will. They just quietly take care of it. They do not bring up issues they see unless specifically asked and will reserve their opinions unless solicited. Workers are reliable, good to have on your team, conscientious, and tend to work well with others.

The future of a Worker is solid. They are not your movers and shakers. They are slow and steady and move up in the organization the same way – slow and steady.

Solvers

Solvers are the employees that everyone wants on their team. They complete all the tasks assigned to them like a Tasker. They do their jobs well like a Worker, and bring up concerns, but Solvers go one step further and offer solutions to the concerns they raise. They see problems as opportunities to fix things. Once given the autonomy, Solvers will fix issues before they are even brought up, so by the time their boss is updated, the situation has already been addressed.

The future of the Solver is bright. Solvers are your managers and directors; they are the movers and the shakers. Solvers are the first ones considered for promotions and raises, and are kept through restructures. Managers will fight to keep them from going to other companies.

Caution: Extreme Solvers
Solvers can go too far and jeopardize their standing. Taken in the extreme, solvers can become overbearing and irritating know-it-alls. They can disrupt a team by not allowing others to have a say or by moving too quickly for others to keep up. Extreme solvers may become braggarts and be perceived as arrogant. Instead of a positive attribute, people taking solving to an extreme can instead orchestrate their own downfalls.

Which Are You?

Which do you tend to be? A Whiner, a Tasker, a Worker, or a Solver? Take the quiz below to help give you some insight.

1. There is a piece of trash in the lobby of your office building. You:
   - A. Do not see the trash; observation is not one of your strong suits.
   - B. Pick up the trash and throw it away, thinking nothing more about it.
   - C. Pick up the trash and start thinking of a process to ensure no more trash finds its way into the lobby.
   - D. Let the manager over the cleaning crew know they are performing sub-par.

2. For the third time this week your computer freezes up. You:
   - A. Call the IT department and take a break, there is nothing you can do about it anyway.
   - B. Create a list of all the things you were working on each time it froze to find a pattern, work with the IT department to fix, then share the findings with your peers.
   - C. Turn your computer off then back on sending a note to the boss that IT is failing to maintain the systems.
   - D. Call IT and remain available to ensure you can answer any questions they have while working on fixing the system.

3. Newly promoted to Communications Manager, the process coordinator for your company's clients, you:

    A. Continue the way you were shown because that is the process that is expected of you.

    B. Complain to co-workers how tedious and ridiculous the process is.

    C. Determine a way to complete the process in half the time, implement the areas you can and meet with the boss to show the cost benefits of changing the process – even though it means buying a new software database.

    D. Quietly adjust obvious redundancies to make the process better.

4. In a meeting with other managers, one of your peers is presenting issues and solutions they are dealing with in their department. You:

    A. Applaud their fantastic presentation and, after the meeting, let them know you can show them how to add videos directly to their file.

    B. Listen attentively and hope it goes well for them.

    C. Volunteer a person from your department to help out with a cross functional solution.

    D. Speak up during their presentation to ask if they considered the fact their solution is too costly.

5. When asked for volunteers to help out with your Company's nonprofit foundation you:

A. Cannot afford the extra time outside of work, but sign up to give feedback for ideas.

B. Explain to the boss that it is unrealistic to ask employees to give their time when most people already work overtime as it is.

C. Work to create ways people can be a part of the process that can fit into any amount of time they have.

D. Don't have time for one more activity on your plate, working takes enough time out of your schedule.

6. While taking notes on actions to send to your department during a meeting between two Vice Presidents, you:

A. Explain that the solution they are thinking about will negatively impact the morale of the employees and you would suggest they come up with a different solution.

B. Bring up the fact that you can pull all the information they are seeking using your computer skills, saving countless hours of manual compilation.

C. Continue to listen and write down take-aways, this discussion is above your paygrade.

D. Figure if they want your opinion they will ask for it, and then you will let them know your ideas.

7. In an advertising meeting you notice the leader has completely lost control of the room. You:

A. Get your information ready based on what has already been suggested and have it ready at the end of the meeting to turn in.

   B. Don't' worry about it, you are getting paid either way.

   C. Let the person know sitting next to you what a waste of time these meetings are.

   D. Stand up, go to the front of the room and call everyone's attention back to the leader.

8. Prior to boarding a plane for a business trip, you realize the plane ride would be a good time to cover information with the boss. You:

   A. After arriving at the destination, chat with the boss of the wasted work time on the plane.

   B. Ask the person next to you if they would be willing to switch seats so you can sit next to the boss.

   C. Look at your seat number in hopes you are sitting together.

   D. Make sure to let the booking agent know to put your seats together next flight.

9. When going to use the copy machine you see there is paper jam. You:

   A. Attempt to clear the jam yourself.

   B. Go find the office manager so they can fix it.

   C. Clear the jam yourself and email your peers letting them know not to use card stock in the printer as it jams it.

   D. Let the office manager know that not only is the copier jammed, but people need to get it fixed and not just leave it for others to figure out.

10. While watching a webinar required for your position you:

    A. Notice some areas that were left out or outdated. You compile the correct data and send it to the webinar contact.

    B. Complete the webinar within the time frame asked of you.

    C. Let the boss know what a waste of time the webinar was as the information was outdated.

    D. Take note of what was outdated and look up the accurate information so you know for your job.

Now take score the answers with the key below and count up how many 1's, 2's, 3's, and 4's you have. Multiply the totals by 10 and that is the percent you are of each category.

Quiz Key

#			#			#		
1	A	2	5	A	3	9	A	3
	B	3		B	1		B	2
	C	4		C	4		C	4
	D	1		D	2		D	1
2	A	2	6	A	1	10	A	4
	B	4		B	4		B	2
	C	1		C	2		C	1
	D	3		D	3		D	3
3	A	2	7	A	3			
	B	1		B	2			
	C	4		C	1			
	D	3		D	4			
4	A	3	8	A	1			
	B	2		B	4			
	C	4		C	2			
	D	1		D	3			

	#	%	
1's			Whiner
2's			Tasker
3's			Worker
4's			Solver

The goal is to be 60%-70% Solver and 30-40% Worker, with hopefully only 0-10% of Whiner/Tasker. How did you do?

Why Not a Solver 100% of the time?
- ✓ Time must be spent on a job well done, on being an excellent worker. If a Solver 100% of the time the job may suffer.
- ✓ It is crucial to ascertain the appropriateness of sharing solutions. If the person is not open to solutions, or the timing is not right, the process can still be completed for development, but voicing the solutions may need to wait for a more appropriate forum.
- ✓ People may become irritated by the constant Solver and tune them out.
- ✓ Others may need to create solutions for their own development.

Steps to Become a Solver

Before implementing any solutions, permission may be needed prior. There may be levels of approval required or you may be excluded from the solution discussion, but always have a solution or multiple ideas ready to share when the time comes. With those parameters in mind, here are steps to help become a Solver:

Step One: Look for issues/concerns rather than ignoring them.

Step Two: When an issue/opportunity is discovered, determine its level of urgency:

✓ Immediate: talk with the supervisor right away, even if no solution is apparent. Examples include safety issues, legal violations, and ethical issues, or anything needing attention that cannot wait.

✓ Not immediate: jot it down and think of solutions to the problem.

– If you owned the company what would you do?

– If you had the authority how would you solve it?

– If you cannot think of any ideas, ask friends and family or talk with your peers.

Raising
Concerns:
Be ready
with a
Solution

Step Three: Once there are few possible solutions, try and identify any concerns or pitfalls with each solution.

✓ What adverse effects could be caused by enacting the solution?

✓ How much money or resources would be needed? Are they available?

✓ How many people and how much time does the solution take?

✓ Does the solution require outside resources, for example, permitting or approvals?

✓ Does the solution go against any company values or branding?

If the solution has passed the test so far, next consider:

✓ Is the person open to suggestions?

✓ Is it the right time and place for all involved?

✓ What political ripples will offering the suggestion(s) cause?

Depending on the answers to the above questions, move forward with suggesting the solution, or hold off of another time.

Step Four: Understand the responsibility - you may be asked to take the lead in implementing. Be willing to complete the solution yourself.

Step Five: Talk with your supervisor

✓ Choose a couple of solutions that do not require additional resources or likely result in adverse effects. Bring to the supervisor along with the issue.

✓ Only bring those solutions that either you can execute yourself, or that you would be willing to with the appropriate resources, tools, and approvals.

Step Six: Let it go

8

Emotional Strength

✓ Understand there may be information you are not aware of and your idea may not be implemented.

✓ Use emotional strength then focus on the next idea versus dwelling on one that was not met with approval.

The process of being a Solver can be much simpler than the above basics and be put together in a few moments, or it can also be much more complicated and time consuming. The importance here is to start looking for solutions.

The Political Side of Solutions

When determining whether or not to present a possible solution, keep in mind how the idea will be received. Others may perceive you as trying to take over their project or responsibility and feel the input is inappropriate. They may become antagonistic and defensive, even going so far as to inform you to mind your own business. Others may feel threatened by suggestions if they perceive you as wanting to take their resources or even their job. If choosing to move forward and voice solutions, be sure to couch suggestions as a non-threatening resource rather than a hostile takeover.

Organizational Politics

Keep in mind the politics of the organization. I was asked to create a proposal addressing any concerns within my region along with accompanying solutions. My boss would be presenting my proposal to the Executive VP of the entire Home Depot. As part of developing those that reported to me, I solicited thoughts from my team. One team member, in particular, thought of some great ideas to address the shortfalls. The only problem was it went against the EVP's vision of where he was leading the company. He was leading a simplified approach, removing tasks at the store level so they could help customers without distraction. The insight of my direct report was right on, the fix was a good one, but there was no way I would submit it as a solution because it caused work for the stores - contrary to what the EVP wanted. If I offered up the solution it would communicate to my boss that I was not in tune with, nor was I supporting, the EVP's vision. Not a wise move. We had to come up with a different solution to submit that could be just as effective but within the vision, and therefore garner the support of the EVP.

Also, keep in mind the relationships inside the organization. For example, if a possible solution eliminates the job of the President's brother, rethink it.

What is the Company's Vision?

Write out the company's vision. If unknown, look it up online, go through material, ask others. Company vision is different than a mission statement. The vision is how the mission statement is achieved, the direction the company is going, what the future looks like, the parameters that create the path for forward movement.

What is the Department and/or Boss's Vision?

Find out what the department vision is and, equally important, what the boss's vision is. Knowing this information will help guide how to present solutions.

Solution Ideas

Write down everything that could be fixed or improved. The list does not need to be long. It is fine to have two or ten items. The important aspect is to collect the list.

Now think of solutions, keeping the previous guidelines in mind. Once a solution to each has been thought of, go through the process of feasibility and reception. The next form can be used to get started. Prepare three to five solutions for every issue as a rule of thumb. It gets the mind working beyond the obvious.

Issue

Solution One: [   ]

Adverse Effects?	$$ / Resources

Labor?	Time?	Down Time?	Company Values?
			Y N

Outside Resources?	Person Open?	Correct Forum?
	Y N	

Politcal Ripples, if any?

Next, decide which suggestions are appropriate to take to the boss or other authority figure. No ideas may come up this round. Keep looking. If solutions are created, it is not a bad idea to briefly touch on the rejected solutions and explain why. It gives the boss insight to your thinking beyond the short term fix and looking at a holistic picture of the company.

Keep the discussion brief. Even the solution needs to be communicated quickly, ideally with something in writing that can be looked at and forwarded if additional approval is needed. Remember to let it go emotionally, so if the idea is not implemented the next idea can be a focus rather than dwelling in the past.

Summary

The higher level in a career the more solutions are expected. No longer is pay solely based on just doing tasks and reporting out information. The expectation is to solve issues, to make and implement solutions for the betterment of the company. Employees that provide solutions, even when it is not their job, move up more quickly, have advantages in promotions, and may be kept more often in restructures and/or layoffs than those that do not. Know which category you generally fall into: Whiner (irritant), Tasker (unmotivated), Worker (steady), Solver (up and coming) and work towards having the mindset of a Solver more often than not.

Chapter Thirteen

Be Action Centric

The Effects of Physical Location

I had recently moved to Seattle and found a producer I might work with for a music recording. As I was waiting for the producer to come out of the studio another musician was playing his guitar. He offered me his chair, the only one there, and I politely declined saying I was young and could sit on the ground. It was amazing how quickly I became a fan in his eyes versus a fellow musician. One moment I was an equal the next I was nothing more than an inconsequential groupie simply by physical positioning. I realized my mistake after a few minutes and stood up to adjust the situation. I stated I would like a chair after all. The dynamics shifted and I was once again on equal footing.

Most people do not put very much thought into where to sit. They walk into a room, look around and choose an empty seat. Some may sit near the front of the room because they cannot see very well. Some choose the back of the room or closest to the exit so they can leave quietly and unseen if so desired. To get some insight into natural tendencies, consider high school or college seating preferences. Many people continue to choose the same seats without thinking about it. Choosing a physical location in a room is much more important than most people realize, especially if looking to move up in an organization.

Be in the Action

There is a meeting in a large conference room. Chairs are around the conference table and on the outside of the room. Where do you sit? Where do you feel most comfortable sitting? In a completely unscientific poll I conducted, I found that most men will sit at the conference table, where only about 50% of women will. Of those women who choose the table, most do so in order to have a place to put their paper while taking notes. In Sheryl Sandberg's book *Lean In*, she begins her second chapter with a story about how executive women chose the side chairs verses sitting at the table even when invited to do so, effectively relegating themselves to support roles. At the table is where the action occurs.

When choosing a physical locale in a given situation, choose to be in the action. When in the action there is access to facial expressions, non-verbal communication, as well as physical information shared in the moment. One can see others and be seen by others. One is inside the decision making group rather than becoming peripheral. Gaining information and raising concerns is easier and more effective. Become a participant of the discussion rather than simply an observer.

Now to break this down. Why it is important to think about and make a conscious decision where to sit and how the choice of a seat can actually alter behavior in a meeting.

Scenario One

Jane was asked to come to a meeting last minute. She dropped what she was doing and headed towards the conference room. Trying to be as unobtrusive as possible, since the meeting was already in progress, she slipped quietly through the door and took a seat along the wall. She listened to people discussing the topic, mostly seeing the backs of their heads. Jane knew she needed to really pay attention since she could not see what they were reviewing. She listened attentively and offered a couple of suggestions but it seemed to interrupt the discussion at the table. Half the people had to stop what they were doing to turn around and see who was talking. Unconvinced she had all the information, Jane ceased making any further suggestions. She would chat with her manager after the meeting to fill in the gaps.

Scenario Two

Jane was asked to come to a meeting last minute and headed for the conference room. Instead of slipping in unobtrusively she quietly greeted people and took a chair at the table. Noticing the discussion revolved around handouts, she politely interrupted the meeting to ask for a copy. After getting caught up on the subject Jane made several suggestions some having

10

Listen with
Intent

already been covered prior to her arrival, but because she was in the midst of the action she felt confident that she understood what was going on and continued to make effective and well received suggestions.

These two scenarios have almost exactly the same components, including the same person, but with a significantly different physical positioning and mindset. In the first scenario, Jane does not feel empowered to contribute. She effectively placed herself in a support role and as an observer. Those that are sitting at the table have access to all the information, are facing each other so they can take advantage of non-verbal communication: expression, interest movement, eye movement, when someone has an idea or dissenting view even before vocalization. Jane has become peripheral, unless an action is taken to draw their attention to her or anyone else not sitting at the table. She is automatically at a disadvantage because she does not have all the information. The decisions will be made at the table and mostly without her.

In the second scenario, Jane has placed herself where she can see what is going on, and asked for the information being reviewed, enabling herself to be a decision maker rather than a supporter. The decisions will still be made at the table with the biggest difference being that her input, including non-verbal communication, will be a part of the discussion.

If sitting at the table and jumping into discussion feels extremely uncomfortable, start small. Start by sitting at the table and take copious notes, watch facial expressions and non-verbal communication. See what additional information is gained by being in the action. Or make a simple suggestion as more confidence is gained and move closer to the table. When at the table, contribute.

Here are suggestions to keep in mind when determining location:

- ✓ Stay away from the back of the room where more conversations are happening, and not necessarily ones regarding the meeting topic. Not only is it distracting, vital opportunities to contribute may be missed.

- ✓ Sit near the top decision makers but not right next to them; close enough for them to observe and recognize contributions but far enough away not be at risk of being moved to accommodate someone else. If the meeting is occurring at the front of the room and the decision makers are sitting at the back of the room, I have found it better to sit near the front rather than near them. They will still observe the action and distractions will be limited.

- ✓ Be observant. If the best place to sit is not obvious, watch. See where the movers sit, where the action takes place. File away the information to use in future meetings.

There are situations where choosing to be in a support location is exactly the right place to be. Consider these additional components when determining location.

What is your role in the meeting or event?

If a decision maker, if the outcome of the meeting affects you, your department, or something that you are responsible for – position yourself in the action. Not doing so demonstrates a lack of investment.

If in a support role, taking notes, getting a feel for the team, or an observer, then there is no need to be in the middle of the action. That being said, if there is room, sit where the action is regardless.

Who are the other players at the meeting/venue?

No one wants to get seated and then be asked to move when someone of higher rank joins the meeting. At this point most of the chairs will be filled and only the least desirable options may be left. Find out ahead of time who else will be attending the meeting and consider where they will be sitting. Choose a seat in the action but not at the risk of being moved.

Meeting Layouts

Here are some example room layouts to get started. Remember, determining the best location in any given situation is based on the individual circumstances. If only at the meeting or venue to learn information and there is no participation or conversation involved, choose a support location.

 Action   Support

Conference Room

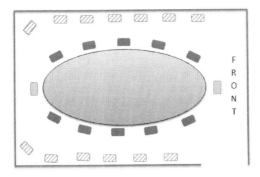

- ✓ Action Role: around the table but not at the head or foot unless leading the meeting
- ✓ Rationale: see all expressions and non-verbals, to see what is happening on the table and to be seen
- ✓ Support Role: around the outside of the room, but if there is room, sit at table

Small Room, Straight Tables

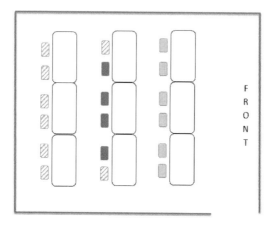

- ✓ Action Role: middle of the 2nd row
- ✓ Rationale: close enough to the front to be engaged, in the middle of people to hear them and gauge reactions
- ✓ Support role: at the back or on the side

Table Pods

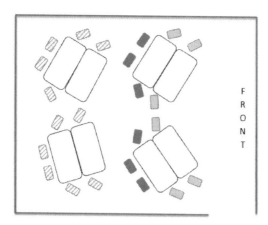

- ✓ Action Role: in the middle of the room at the front two tables
- ✓ Rationale: If right up front there is less engagement with how others are feeling or what discussions are occurring
- ✓ Support: at the back

U Shaped Tables

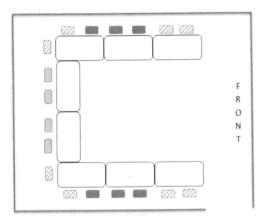

- ✓ Action: second table back from the front
- ✓ Rationale: the best place to be able to see everyone, close to the leader(s) which tend to sit at the back tables
- ✓ Support: either at the back table or the first tables closest to the front

Classroom Style

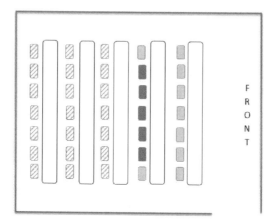

- ✓ Action: second or third row from the front depending on the size of the room (third if large room)
- ✓ Rationale: the first row hinders engagement with the rest of the participants - staying near the front enhances focus, is closer to the speaker, while still hearing the conversations
- ✓ Support: closer to the back and the edges

Roadblocks

All of this positioning sounds great, but let's real world this. One does not get the luxury of choosing where to sit at every event. Although some roadblocks cannot be overcome, a little bit of foresight can go a long way.

Be Early

Most roadblocks are removed if arriving early to every meeting. Not only are there more options of where to sit, but time can be taken to consider placement based on the room layout and acoustics. If arriving on time versus early, it is guaranteed others have already chosen seats to their best advantage or comfort. Be early rather than on time.

If arriving early is not a possibility, because of other meetings or calls, consider reserving a place prior to the other call/meeting. Ask another colleague to save a place or adjust the time of the previous meeting, if its content is not as important.

Called in After the Meeting Starts

Most likely the best seats have already been taken, if called into a meeting already in progress. It is important to know how long you will be needed: for a few minutes or for the rest of the meeting. If only for a few minutes remain standing while learning what is needed.

If remaining in the meeting for its entirety, I suggest to remain standing at first, just inside the door, and scope out the room. After ascertaining the most advantageous place to sit, only then, choose a seat. If the outskirt of the room is the only option, consider using the chair as a place to put papers but remain standing. It is the best way not to become peripheral and be able to see the most what is happening, and the easiest position to jump in and add thoughts. By standing, you remind everyone you are there. Remember to have an open, non-aggressive posture.

Assigned Seating

Graciously accept the proffered seat and make the best of it. Stay focused and interact. Use participation to state presence.

Asked to Move

No matter how careful the planning, there is always the possibility that a chair change occurs. When having to move, accept the move with grace and move to a location that is still relevant. Stand if necessary.

Leading a Meeting

If leading a meeting, it is a good idea to determine seating ahead of time. Where to sit as a leader, just as a participant, depends on what outcome is desired. What is the purpose of the meeting?

For example, if hosting but others are speaking, choose a support location. If speaking, be at the front of the room or at the head of the table, smack dab in the middle of the action. If the only one speaking, choose a location that is the easiest to be seen and heard by all.

Here are more suggestions to help in determining location as a leader depending on the role.

Leader Positioning

Purpose / Role	Example
Facilitator	You have coordinated the meeting, but have others that are guest speakers
Seating Suggestion	**Rationale**
Sit at the very back or side back of the room, coming forward to introduce the next guest.	Be a support role and do not distract from the focus of the meeting
Purpose / Role	**Example**
Observer	Others are running the meeting and your role is to see how others perform
Seating Suggestion	**Rationale**
Very back of the room	Do not draw attention; blend into the background giving the best opportunity to truly observe
Purpose / Role	**Example**
Speaker / Leader	You are the main speaker / leader
Seating Suggestion	**Rationale**
Right in the middle of the action. If doing a presentation be at the front of the room with the presentation; stand do not sit; if a table sit at the head of the table so you can see everyone	Keep your presence known and the focus on what you are doing/saying/presenting. Standing is more powerful then sitting if at the front of a room.
Purpose / Role	**Example**
Brainstorming	You are looking for ideas from everyone and want to draw out solutions
Seating Suggestion	**Rationale**
Either be at the front of the room as the writer of the ideas, or have someone else write the ideas and sit intermingled with the group	If the facilitator of the brainstorm, then be at the front of the room to direct. If someone else is the facilitating, blend so others feel comfortable contributing.

Other Venues

Not all meetings are in relatively small rooms; some have no chairs; some include unknown players. As a general rule choose a position to be able to contribute, be engaged and to be recognized.

I recently attended a Women's Conference hoping for some great networking while not having an active role in the conference itself. I had a few objectives when choosing a seat:

1) To see the stage and the people speaking
2) A friend was speaking and I wanted to be of service in case she needed anything
3) Be in a position to network with others
4) Able to exit without being distracting
5) Up front where I could be seen by all others, but still able to see a bit of the room

Seating was at round tables which held about six women each. I chose the very front table closest to the stage (#1) and the seat at the table closest to the edge by the exit door. I ended up needing to be in that location as I videoed a friend's presentation from my iPad (#2). Other speakers noticed (#5) and asked if I would film them as well giving me good networking (#3). I ended up having to use the restroom during a presentation so was able to exit without disrupting (#4). It was a great choice!

Stand Up Meetings

A meeting called where there are no chairs and everyone is standing, like in a tour or tradeshow, is a good place to be front and center to see what is transpiring. If being noticed is not a goal, being in the middle of the group is a good choice. The very back communicates avoidance where an edge can communicate being supportive, allowing others to have a better view. I suggest only taking the edge or back position if the content is already known or if fulfilling a support role where the information is not as impactful, giving others better earshot. If a participant, being up front shows engagement and focus. The back holds more distractions and it is easy to miss what is being communicated.

Training Class or Conference

Sit close to the trainer in order to get as much information as possible, usually this means at the front of the room. Sitting at the front helps one stay focused with fewer distractions from others, gives better access to the trainer for questions, and allows non-verbal cues to reach the trainer which could adjust the pace and detail they use.

No Seating Mixer

At venues where there is no seating, but people stand or walk around, again, determine the purpose at the venue. If trying to meet people, walk around versus standing in one place. If some time is needed to create a plan, choose a place on the edges of the event with a good vista, decide whom you would like to speak with and start mingling.

Restaurant

If there are quite a few people eating together where a very long table is utilized, there are different dynamics at each location of the table. Again, what is the purpose of being there and/or what is the desired outcome of the event?

If there is a particular person you want to have access to, try and sit across from them or at an angle where you can be a part of the conversations they are having. Sitting right next to is not ideal but okay if sitting across is not feasible. Sitting across allows an easy conversation without excluding others.

If being in the action is the goal, but without a specific person to chat with, sit as close to the middle of the table as possible. It provides the best chance of interacting with the most people.

If fulfilling a support role only, not needed for any specific conversation, then sit at the end of the table.

Wherever I sit, I usually get up and walk around to touch base with others at the table before the meal is served or at the end when others have moved so I can be a part of their conversation if only for a few minutes. That way I am still able to interact with everyone even in a seated table environment.

Summary

Look for the action seats when choosing a physical location.

✓ Understand the dynamics of the people and purpose of the meeting and determine the location that will provide the best setting in which to participate.

✓ Be pro-active in reducing or overcoming roadblocks by arriving at events or meetings early.

✓ Pro-actively select a location, rather than stumbling into it, so the best opportunity to add value, gather information, and have a successful outcome is possible.

Chapter Fourteen

Be Promotable

The Basics

In order to be promotable, all the basics of the job must be covered and beyond:

- ✓ Do the job well

- ✓ Stand out as a dependable employee

- ✓ Be on time

- ✓ Contribute high quality work

- ✓ Be a solver with minimal complaining

- ✓ Complete requests with a sense of urgency

- ✓ Be viewed as a leader

- ✓ Be competent to take on additional responsibilities

- ✓ Have a good attitude

- ✓ Welcome new challenges

If the above does not describe you, then work on these areas first before proceeding. Many chapters in this book provide pointers and ideas to help achieve the goal of being promotable.

If the above list does describe you and you are still not getting promoted, then here are a few places to start.

Check Your History

Have you been offered opportunities but turned them down? If you have turned down several opportunities extended, you may be designated as un-promotable. A colleague of mine was so focused on what he wanted in his career path he turned down three promotions with other departments. He was no longer considered for *any* promotions. The path to achieve a goal is rarely straight; experience in other areas can be extremely helpful in achieving the goal, even if does not make sense at the time.

Be open-minded to moving where the job leads, taking advantage of the opportunities that arise. If not able to seize an opportunity, be specific as to why (for example, relocating is not possible until the children graduate high school, which is three years away). Giving a specific reason creates a temporary decline versus the impression of disinterest. As a general rule, if promotional offers are rejected three times, future promotions may cease to be offered.

Ask for and Act on Feedback

There may be something missing either in leadership style or interactions with others. Is there a blind spot where some objective feedback is needed? Was there feedback given in the past that was not acted upon? First, look back at previous reviews or any other feedback given specifically from the boss or other authority figure. Has there been positive movement in those areas? If not, start there.

Depending on the size of the company there may be formal programs available, such as a 360 survey. If so, ask to be a part of one.

Ask the boss to give feedback as well as peers and direct reports. Create a questionnaire for them to answer if one is not available. I have created a simple feedback form that can be used, or create one that is more tailored to what specific feedback is desired. It is good, whichever form or questions are used, to communicate in such a way that allows participants to feel comfortable giving truthful answers. There are two ways to do this, both of which I suggest are done simultaneously.

Make the
Most of
Feedback

Make it Anonymous

Utilize apps with a link that people can enter information anonymously.

Not as confidential, but worth trying if an app or other software program is not feasible, is to go through a trusted person in the office or facility or better yet, create a box where participants can drop their feedback into. If going through a person, they all give to that person who then compiles the information and no handwriting is seen. If using a box, suggest everyone type their responses so identities are kept confidential.

Ask Your Questions Two Levels Up

Ask people to answer feedback questions focused on two levels up in the organization. People may not feel comfortable answering what your opportunities are now as they see them. Most will feel comfortable projecting out several years and will in turn be more honest.

Simple Feedback Request

Circle Relationship: Peer   Report   Business Partner   Boss

1. What do I need to work on in order to achieve two levels higher in our organization than I am currently?

2. What do I do well and excel in currently?

3. Where have I improved in the most over the past 6-12 months?

Be Approachable

2

Be Approachable

Being absolutely fantastic in executing the job is not enough. One must also be approachable. Many detail oriented and efficient people have this opportunity. Their mind and attention is so focused on the project or task at hand that people take a back seat. The unapproachable person tends to dive right into the topic at hand with nary a hello or first asking about the other person's day. Because this person can be so focused, others may be reticent to interrupt their rapt attention and tend to walk by instead of engaging.

A person with a high level of intensity and high level of knowledge and expertise can be intimidating to others. It is important in this case to reach out and put others at ease.

Research Promotional Job Requirements

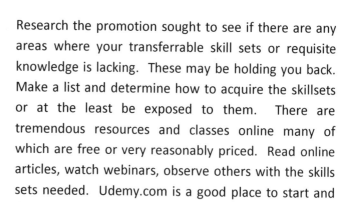

Research the promotion sought to see if there are any areas where your transferrable skill sets or requisite knowledge is lacking. These may be holding you back. Make a list and determine how to acquire the skillsets or at the least be exposed to them. There are tremendous resources and classes online many of which are free or very reasonably priced. Read online articles, watch webinars, observe others with the skills sets needed. Udemy.com is a good place to start and they have specials that bring the prices down.

Get Exposure

Know who makes the decisions on promotions and get exposure to those people. If the decision makers do not know who you are and what you have to offer they will, nine times out of ten, choose a person they know – even if on paper you look better. Be vigilant in finding out who those decision makers are and be a part of meetings, facility visits, projects, and conversations with them. If no opportunities are found at first, keep looking to take advantage of opportunities that present themselves in the future. Always be ready.

Do Parts of the Job Now

If it is possible, start doing aspects of the desired position now. When I was a waitress, working through college, I applied for a trainer position and was almost laughed out of the interview. They did not see me as trainer material. I decided that the next time the position opened up I would get it. So I started looking at my position a little differently. If I was a trainer, what would I do? I began doing extra little things to help my fellow servers, clear a table if I was not busy, help other tables if they needed it even though not in my station, pick up trash, be the first to volunteer to help with large tables, help others with their side work, and the like. Three months later another trainer position became available and I received the promotion.

When I was an HR Analyst I was helping out a manager who had been given the specialty areas (Kitchens/Flooring/Millwork) as an additional assignment. She met with me every few weeks to see what kind of data and analysis I could provide. Rather than just giving her reports for what she requested I approached the project as if I was over the area. I provided what I would want to see as a manager. The manager over the project was crazy busy with her own job and basically relied on me to do all the behind the scenes work. Little did I realize how important this experience would be when my analyst position was eliminated. With this experience, I was able to receive a promotion to Regional Specialty Manager. Even when not aware of it, expanding in the current job role may result in positive effects down the road.

Get on a Project Team that Interacts with the Position

A great way to get exposure to the people making decisions, as well as others in the department, is to work directly with them. Interesting enough, there are times where people think they want a position, but once they see what really goes on or see firsthand the politics of the department, they change their mind. The grass is not always greener on the other side. That being said, exposure to the people in the desired department is a great way to have an in when an opportunity arises. In the meantime, it expands business understanding and increases networking.

If a project team is not a possibility, look at what is currently being done and see if there can be any synergy created by including another person's thoughts from another department. The findings might be surprising.

Check Social Media Accounts

Nothing spells disaster on the work front faster than incriminating photos or discussions on social media sites. In today's fast paced electronic information age, what is done in private seldom remains so if it is floating out there in cyber-space. The adage "my personal life is separate from business" only works if not subscribing to *any* social media which include personal aspects. Go through all social media accounts and see if there are any incriminating photos from a perception standpoint, not your perception, anyone's perception. Ask a trusted person with social media savvy to test your internet presence. It might be surprising what they find.

A respected friend and colleague of mine had posted a photo of herself with a glass of wine from a celebration. She was not intoxicated, not at work, but the backlash she received from that photo was very negative. People began talking about her behind her back, wondering if she was an alcoholic, commenting she made a poor judgement call. Some became more guarded with her. It began to encroach on her professional life and she ended up making the decision to take the picture down. Be careful what you post. The simplest and most innocuous photo can take on a meaning of its own. Check accounts and limit connections.

Human resource professionals, loss prevention, and investigations even for potential promotions may look at social media as one set of information points. Only post what is appropriate for anyone to see no matter what the context.

Communicate Goals

Sadly, I have seen many people passed over for promotions because the decision makers did not know they wanted the job. As a consequence they were not even considered. Many times job openings are not widely communicated. Be sure that others know about your goals. If a supportive boss knows what your goals are they can help you achieve them faster. Many times a boss will tailor feedback towards achieving that next position.

Market Yourself

17

Market Yourself

Are the decision makers aware of your work? Does the boss understand all you contribute? Unless you have ensured he/she knows of your accomplishments, there may be crucial aspects of your skills sets that have either gone unnoticed or have not had the opportunity to shine. It is up to you to communicate what you do and how you are positively contributing to the betterment of the company.

Dress for the Part

Perception is the reality of decision making and one must take the perception of others into the equation. As surface as it appears, dressing for the part is a necessary step. Undertake a little research. What style of clothing do other people in the job wear? If a suit, then start wearing a suit even if that is not the style of your current job. If wearing a baseball cap but no one in that department wears one, then stop wearing a baseball cap – at least at work.

I am not suggesting a complete wardrobe make over or to spend thousands of dollars to wear the exact name brand of the most successful person in the position. Dressing for the part means that others, specifically the decision makers, can see you fitting into the department, can see you taking on the role. Dress can be a subtle aspect of the decision, but do not be fooled into thinking it is unimportant. People are judged by the way they are dressed, unjustified as the end result of that judgment is. Sharp dressers are considered more competent, sloppy dressers are considered less engaged. That may be the complete opposite of reality, but perception is the basis of decision making. One of the perceptions comes from dress. Take advantage of it!

✓ Wear pressed clothes or have clothes professionally laundered, if appropriate.

- ✓ Do not wear clothes with any stains on them; pretending the stains occurred at work is a poor plan.

- ✓ Ensure shoes look good.
  - o Do not wear old shoes with scuffs and wear marks.
  - o Keep polished if applicable
  - o Match the color/style to your clothing

- ✓ Ensure hair is neat and trimmed and in some sort of style.
  - o If you color your hair, have a regularly scheduled maintenance plan.
  - o Keep hair conditioned and looking healthy.

- ✓ Unless it is part of the job, do not wear revealing clothes – it detracts from appearing competent

- ✓ If you have pierced ears, wear earrings; you look unfinished without them. Studs are fine.

- ✓ Match handbags and purses to the outfit; a neutral color that goes with everything can keep it simple.

Look at and Take Pictures

Find pictures of yourself in your work environment or better yet ask someone to take pictures over the next two weeks while you are at work. Then review the photos. Is the outfit sharp? Pressed? Clean? Stain free? Professional? If you did not know what your job was, by the pictures alone, what would you imagine it to be? Do you exude confidence? Are you happy? Are you welcoming? What is your expression?

Make adjustments as needed, then do the exercise again and review. Have you made progress?

Film Yourself

There is no faster way to see behaviors needing to be adjusted than to be filmed. It does not need to be fancy, a smartphone or tablet can be quite effective. Film yourself in a meeting, during a presentation or other work venue. How do you come across? What works well? What needs to be changed? Work on changing noticeable areas then repeat the process to confirm progress.

I was featured in a human interest story about my music writing and recording. The camera crew followed me around for a few hours while I worked, interviewed me, and filmed while I recorded at a music studio. I received all the raw footage. Watching the footage I was appalled at some irritating quirks I saw and realized not all my clothes fit me as well I thought they did. I was able to make immediate adjustments to both my wardrobe and the quirks that were unbecoming.

Personal Hygiene is Paramount

I knew a woman who was fantastic at her job, great with people, had excellent knowledge and experience, but always had chipped and unkempt nails, dye marks in her hair, and her teeth stained from smoking along with food bits in them. It was very difficult for people to see beyond the surface when distracted by the lack of personal hygiene. As simple and obvious as this sounds check your hygiene. Too many talented and amazing people have been passed over because of it.

- ✓ Bathe or shower *every* day and wear some sort of deodorant.

- ✓ Wash your hair every day – hair traps scent and collects oils.

- ✓ Check your hands, make sure they are manicured (no hang nails, nails trimmed, if polished no chips, clean nail).

- ✓ If dry skin is a problem – use lotion, do not allow it to flake off.

- ✓ Make sure teeth are clean.
  - ○ Check in the morning before leaving for work
  - ○ Check every time after eating
  - ○ Floss – there is nothing more distracting (except that piece of spinach from lunch) than to see

> unhealthy, plaque ridden gums and teeth – keep them clean
>   - o Carry breath mints or gum and use them

- ✓ Make sure your face is washed – no sleep or gummies in your eyes.

- ✓ If wearing makeup, make sure it is fresh.
    - o Have a light touch; makeup should enhance verses detract.
    - o Do not allow mascara to clump.
    - o Check to ensure there is no makeup line between your face and neck.

- ✓ If a smoker, I suggest you quit. It is healthier for you. If quitting is not an option, I suggest you *not* smoke in your house or car. Even if you cannot smell the stale aftereffects, everyone around you can. It is very offensive to smell like an ashtray. Smoke outside in order to keep clothing as well as yourself clean and fresh.

- ✓ Have a light hand on the cologne. If you can smell it, it is too much. Do not try and cover up the smell of something else with it. The two scents mix, rarely making a good combination. Get rid of the other smell at the source rather than trying to cover it up.

Outside Impacts

There are times when, no matter how amazing and deserving of a promotion or an opportunity, you are passed by. Sometimes these decisions have nothing to do with you personally either positive or negative. Promotions may be given because of a previous relationship, nepotism, office politics, blackmail, or any other number of reasons. Sometimes the organization may not be the best fit for your skillsets or potential. The person making the decisions may be intimidated by you or they are afraid of competition.

Whatever the reason, understand that you may be doing everything exactly right. In this case, action may need to be taken by looking for an opportunity outside the company.

Summary

There are a variety of reasons that may be hindering a promotion. To create the best chance, be open minded to shortfalls and take action to change. It may take a little while for others to see the results so make these positive changes as a life behavior and not only as a means to an end. Change must be genuine for others to acknowledge it.

Chapter Fifteen

The Secrets of Effective Game Plans

The secrets of effective game plans, strategies, and solutions can be applied to almost any situation that requires more than a single directive. This is a learned skill and possibly a different way to think. Those who struggle the most in reading through this chapter are probably those with the greatest need of the process. Stick with it. The path outlined in this chapter is a tried and true method for creating effective game plans. It can positively change the course of a career.

The Secrets

Determine a goal and the measure of success. Then:

Secret #1:   Believe You are Impactful

Believe that personal actions will impact the future outcome of a situation and then: *act on that belief.*

Secret #2:   Create Multi-Faceted Solutions

Once equipped with the mindset of an impactful person, the next step is to create the solutions or components for the game plan. The secret here is to brainstorm as many ideas as possible, then choose five to implement.

Secret #3:   Apply the Word "How"

For each component in the game plan, apply the word "How" until there are ideally five, and possibly more, tangible actions listed that can be implemented (at the very least there must be three). The number of actions will depend on the complexity of the component. Questioning each component also shows how viable the idea is: is it good to keep or does it need to be altered or discarded and another component take its place?

Secret #4:   Create Actions along with Due Dates

Word each action in a specific and measurable way so direction is clear; the answer when determining completion is: Yes, No, or Circumstances Changed. Give every action a specific due date. Dates such as "ongoing" or "every week" are not an option.

Next Steps: Implement and Follow Up

Start implementing the actions of the components. Create follow up intervals to check completion and needed adjustments.

Case Study

I was discussing this process with a client of mine, Gwen, and she decided to see how it worked on a personal goal. Part way through the process she became stuck so I walked her through the steps. Here is what happened.

The Goal: To lose weight

Success Measure: To weigh 135 pounds

#2 Create Multiple Solutions

Gwen tried to think of multiple solutions or components for her goal of losing weight. She could only come up with three and became stuck.

As we chatted on the phone, she said, "I can't think of any more, and I am supposed to come up with five?? There aren't any more!"

Goal
Lose Weight

Success Outcome	Final weight of 135 lbs

Brainstorm Ideas

1. Eat a healthly 1400 cal / day
2. Exercise 6 days week
3. Substitute water for food cravings

"Think of this as a brainstorm," I responded, "come up with as many ideas as possible even if they are silly or unreasonable, or even unfeasible. Write them down anyway. The idea here is to create ideas that may springboard to other ideas."

My response was met by silence. So I started asking her questions:

- ✓ "What do you enjoy?"

- ✓ "What motivates you?"

- ✓ "What activities do others do?"

- ✓ "Where else can you find help?"

- ✓ "What can be done right where you are?"

Then she started rattling off ideas and added ten more to her original three in less than three minutes. I did not give her any specifics just asked her questions to help get her mind started. It is very helpful to solicit the ideas of others, even if they are simply a sounding board.

	Brainstorm Ideas
1	Eat a healthly 1400 cal / day
2	Exercise 6 days/week
3	Substitute water for food cravings
4	Collect inspirational images
5	Talk to doctor about my goals
6	Enlist friends' help with exercise, diet, ideas
7	Play music for movement
8	No more house keeper
9	Garden
10	Active home improvement
11	Get up earlier
12	Get more sleep
13	Find and take up a sport
14	
15	

From this list I asked her to decide on five components to include in her game plan. Many times the brainstorm itself will create actions for the next phase. She chose:

Components	
1	Eat a healthly 1400 cal / day
2	Exercise 6 days week
3	Collect inspirational images
4	Enlist the help of others
5	Change Schedule

#3 Apply the Word "How"

At first, the only action Gwen could think of was to track her calorie intake by using an app through her phone. So I asked, "How else?"

"Well, that should pretty much do it," she answered.

"You need to set yourself up for success," I said, "If you cannot articulate the actual process you will undertake then you have less of a chance of actually accomplishing your goal. You need more actions detailing how you will actually achieve eating 1400 calories per day consistently. Keep asking how."

- ✓ How do you know your meals will add up to 1400 each day?
- ✓ How do you ensure you are getting balanced meals?
- ✓ How do you set yourself up with a checkpoint?
- ✓ How do you educate yourself if needed?
- ✓ How do you set yourself up to be successful?

After considering the questions Gwen began adding additional actions.

Solution Component
Eat a healthly 1400 cal / day

	How will you accomplish it?
Action	Track my caloric intake
Action	Get ideas for meal planning
Action	Review literature for education
Action	Plan meals weekly
Action	Follow up to see if I did each item

#4 Create Actions Along Due Dates

Action Wording

Our dialogue continued. "So we have some good actions to start with. Now it is time to get more specific with the wording. These actions are ambiguous. Be very clear on what you are doing and can follow up with each on a specific date with one of the following answers: Yes, No, Circumstances Changed."

Gwen was a little confused, "How do we do that? I think they are fine the way they are."

"Let's look at the first one," I answered. "What will you use to track your calories? When will you start? For how long?"

"Okay, I see," said Gwen. "I need to be more specific. I will use an online App because it will be on my phone and I can access it anywhere."

"Great! Update the wording. Let's keep going. Where are you looking for meal planning and what literature will you use for education?"

Gwen began rewording the actions so they were tangible and gave her a specific map outlining what and how she would accomplish the component.

Solution Component
Eat a healthly 1400 cal / day

	How will you accomplish it?
Action	Use Calorie King to track calorie intake for one month
Action	Review first line therapy for meal planning
Action	Review Covert Baily's literature
Action	Design weekly menu plans every Sunday for shopping that week
Action	Create checkbox to determine if I prepared and ate the food on the menu plan, update daily, review trends weekly

"Gwen, look at the difference between the wording of your first actions versus these! What do you see?"

"I can do each of these," Gwen said. "I have an actual path and specifics that I can accomplish!" A light in her eyes showed me she not only understood the process but that it would work in helping her be successful.

Action Dates

Realistic
Estimations

"Now we need to add in dates when you will start or finish each one of these."

"But they are on-going, how can I put dates on them?" asked Gwen.

"When will you get the online app and begin using it?" I countered, "and for how long will you do it?"

"Oh, I see. I will download the app this week, and will start using it next week."

"Great, add the dates in." I kept going, "When will you review the meal planning and the literature?"

"Got it," replied Gwen, and she proceeded to fill in the dates for her actions.

Solution Component		
Eat a healthly 1400 cal / day		

	How will you accomplish it?	Due Date	Complete?
Action	Use Calorie King to track calorie intake for one month	Start 31-Aug	
Action	Review first line therapy for meal planning	26-Jul	
Action	Review Covert Baily's literature	31-Jul	
Action	Design weekly menu plans every Sunday for shopping that week	26-Jul	
		2-Aug	
		9-Aug	
		16-Aug	
		23-Aug	
Action	Create checkbox to determine if I prepared and ate the food on the menu plan, update daily, review trends weekly	2-Aug	
		9-Aug	
		16-Aug	
		23-Aug	

Gwen felt comfortable with the process after we worked through it step by step and was able to complete the rest of the actions for each component on her own.

Next Steps

Now it is time to implement the game plan or strategy.

- ✓ Check all actions and due dates with a calendar to ensure they are feasible and adjust if necessary.

- ✓ Put all actions on a calendar to include reminders for a higher rate of success.

- ✓ Set times to follow up on progress.

- ✓ Be willing to adjust if an action or component of the solution is not working.

Additional Resources

Secret #1:   Believe You Are Impactful

Personal belief is critical. Beliefs have amazing creative power. When that power is released, willingness and courage to think outside the box follow. This creates a welcoming environment for ideas to arise from unexpected places and gives the subconscious permission to get involved. True belief is absolutely necessary to move forward. Otherwise one can feel like an imposter, doubt the ideas that come to mind, not fully commit the resources and time to see the solution through to fruition. With true belief comes passion and determination and confident knowledge of making a difference.

Humans, and especially women, continuously underestimate the effects of personal impact on the end result of a given situation. Even deciding not to act creates impact. Lack of action as well as purposeful action will impact the course of business. It is a fact. When a mindset changes from observer and reporter to participant and solver, the actions and ideas created change as well. This mindset change spurs the brain to creativity because now there is co-responsibility for the outcome. Now the personal impact affects the result.

If You Do not Feel Impactful

 Drop something small in a still body of water and watch the ripples.

 Get a plant for your desk. It is completely your impact that determines if it lives, dies, or thrives.

 Think about your jobs either at work or home. If you stopped doing them, how would it affect those around you?

 Start with something small you control that impacts others and you believe would work better if a small change occurred – then make that change. How did it affect others?

 Look for ways you can lend an idea or resource to a project or goal the boss, another colleague, or department is working on. Follow how it impacts the final outcome. Remember, sometimes an idea is not used but was necessary in order to get to the final idea and was foundational in the success of the overall goal.

Think Back...

...over the past week and make a list of the different concerns or desired changes the company or department dealt with both big and small.

- ✓ How did you mentally react to each?

- ✓ Did you think you could make any impact on any of them?

- ✓ Did you feel powerless or powerful to adjust the outcome?

- ✓ Did you volunteer any ideas or solutions?

- ✓ Did you think someone else would handle them?

- ✓ Did you wait for others to come up with ideas?

- ✓ What was your mindset?

- ✓ What were your thoughts?

For each item on your list write down what your mental response was.

- ✓ Do you see a pattern?

- ✓ Do you like the pattern?

Real Time

Do the same exercise in real time. When an outcome needs to change or the company has a goal or needs a solution, jot down the topic, observe what your reactions are, and write them down. Next, think of ways to impact the outcome.

Secret #2:   Create Multi-Faceted Solutions

When looking to change an outcome or achieve a goal, the first two ideas are usually the most evident surface concepts. They take little time and creativity to create. They are also usually necessary and obvious and many times the foundation from which other components of the solution or strategy must be built upon. The key here is to keep thinking, creating, and adding components to the strategy.

Pushing past the first few obvious ideas usually takes some digging, some brainstorming, gathering resources and perceptions from others; allowing the subconscious to mull over the situation and suggest ideas while in the shower or other place it can get attention. Push past the first few ideas and commit to having as many as possible (try for a dozen or even twenty five!). This is where the unearthed jewels are found, the genius. Ideas given time to incubate tend to be the most powerful, intriguing, and effective.

> **Brainstorming**: a process where ideas are allowed to be shared with no filters or judgement. This process allows the brain to flow and spark ideas from other ideas. Brainstorming can be done alone but gets easier and usually more productive when done with a group.

As these new ideas are created, many of them will naturally begin to fit into categories and provide some really good components. Some of the ideas themselves will become actions under the components.

After collecting as many ideas as possible, review and determine the best five (minimum of three). Choose components that approach the solutions from different perspectives. Not every component of a solution will be effective. The more diverse the components are, the more probability of success. Limiting the number of components to five is to limit complexity and becoming overwhelmed. If a component is not as effective as needed, switch it out for another rather than trying every idea from the onset.

Practice

Write down a goal or end result to achieve today. Keep it small and simple for this exercise. Now list five or more ways to approach the situation in order to affect the outcome. Keep pushing to come up with at least five ideas, even after you seem to have exhausted them. Get other people's thoughts; allow the mind to sift through them.

Practice More

Continue to practice as opportunities arise. The simple questions: "How Else?" or "What is another way?" are good to ask. Practicing this mindset and questioning helps prepare for situations that really need it. The discipline of going beyond the obvious is learned and only becomes habit as it is repeated.

Apply

The next time there is an opportunity to brain storm, create a game plan, solution, or strategy – apply this newly learned skill and keep going until there are at least five actionable components.

Secret #3:   Apply the Word "How"

In asking the questions during Secret Three, the idea takes shape, feasibility is determined, adjustments made. At this stage, be open to change. The idea may even be shelved for another time or not used at all based on the answers to the question. The key is to ask the questions *before* implementation, to have a plan based on thought and as many facts and as much forecasting as is reasonable. The more detailed the answers ahead of time, the more successful the implementation.

If unable to answer the question "How?" then it stands to reason that it will also be impossible to implement the idea for there is no direction or action to take. The process does not have to take hours, although it can. I have created solutions and answered the question "How?" in as little as a few minutes for simple solutions and days or weeks for more complex ones.

Secret 4:   Create Actions with Due Dates

The wording of actions is critical. If the question "How" can still be asked, continue to refine and clarify the action. Compare the wording on the examples below from the Case Study. The actions are all the same, but the wording changes to become very specific. When defined specifically, actions have a much greater chance of actually being accomplished.

Before	After
Track my caloric intake	Use Calorie King to track calorie intake for one month
Get ideas for meal planning	Review First Line Therapy for meal planning
Review literature for education	Review Covert Baily's literature
Plan meals weekly	Design weekly menu plans every Sunday for shopping that week
Follow up to see if I did each item	Create checkbox to determine if I prepared and ate the food on the menu plan, update daily, review trends weekly

It is important to word the actions so a finite response can be given as to its completion, as in the example.

Answer	Definition
Yes	The action was completed by the due date
No	The action was not completed by the due date
Circumstances Changed	The action was not able to be completed because of a change in circumstances which could be either outside the individual's control, or a decision was made to specifically not continue with the action.

Wording actions specifically and with corresponding due dates is crucial to ensure actions are truly actionable verses being vague. Taking the time to commit to the process but leaving out the time frame, may result in work that is completed slower and less effectively.

Worksheets

Next are worksheets to help create effective game plans and strategies. Once the concepts and flow are familiar, any blank piece of paper, or electronic writing will work. Some people are so good at this process they can work it out in their minds. The important part is to commit to the process and watch new creative ideas and movement flow!

Game Plan Brainstorm

List the goal. Be specific on what will be accomplished along with any accompanying numbers or metrics that will measure success. For example, if trying to increase sales – by how much? Trying to raise awareness of a product – what is the gauge for success? By the number of likes on your page? Be specific about what is being changed or achieved.

Game Plan Components

Choose the five components to implement.

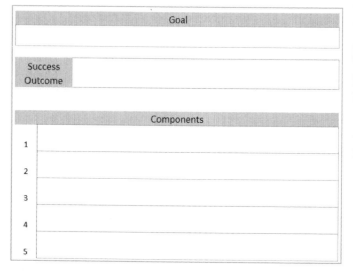

Game Plan Actions

Use one worksheet for each component in the game plan. Ensure actions are very specific, providing a clear action plan.

Solution Component			
How will you accomplish it?		Due Date	Complete?
Action			
Action			
Action			
Action			
Action			

Must have at least three steps/ways - forces you to think beyond the obvious.
Each step must be able to be completed by a specific date, no on-going due dates.
When asked if completed, the answers can only be: Yes, No, Circumstances Changed.

Summary

The secrets of effective game plans, strategies, and solutions can be applied to almost any situation requiring more than a single directive. Using this process sets people up for successful execution. The secrets:

	Secrets
One	Believe your actions impact the future outcome of the given situation
Two	Create multi-faceted solutions with ideally five components
Three	Apply the word "How" to each component until tangible actions are created and all questions are answered
Four	Create specific actions with due dates that when determining if complete can be answered with: Yes, No, or Circumstances Changed

Chapter Sixteen

Stay in Motion

Why It is Necessary

I did not realize how the course of my Home Depot career was shaped in a very positive way until it stopped moving. In retrospect, one of the aspects that kept me engaged and growing was the constant change. I did not always like it at the time. The company was growing so quickly that there were structure changes, expansions in positions, and new office openings. In short, there was plenty of opportunity for movement. Looking back, I realize part of the key to my success was this constant motion. I was always learning, challenged, and stretched. I was growing and developing professionally, but was also able to bring a new perspective to each position and create solutions. I worked for many different leaders with various leadership and communication styles. I didn't have the opportunity to get comfortable, to get bored, or to get complacent. Because I stayed in motion, I was able to have a varied and successful career for over twenty one years with the same company.

And then... I stopped moving. I had a total of twelve different roles over the course of two decades. Each position lasted three years or less until my final position as Regional Director of Operations/Asset Protection (RDO). The first three to four years as the RDO I thrived. It was a tough new challenge and, to that date, the hardest job I had experienced bringing all my creative solutions and training and organizational skills to bear. In my last year as a Regional Director I had stagnated. I was no longer challenged (although I still had challenging issues to deal with). Since my interest was no longer piqued, I became less engaged, and when this happens failure is close at hand unless a change is made. It was time to move, to create needed change. So I left the company to start a new chapter.

Change can be scary, but it is that very reality that causes our minds to snap to attention, awareness heightened, and learning revved up. Yes, it is a little stressful, but stress can be good – the kind where excitement is, and curiosity, and interest (versus panic, fear, run for your life kind of stress). Stress can enhance the senses, specifically the brain. Suddenly new perspectives are seen, the brain is challenged and, as long as it is not too much change all at once, the challenge is likely to be met with a sense of accomplishment. As long as there is learning, and growing and expanding, new discoveries of capabilities and personal belief are made. The mind thrives on new things to consider, to ponder, to solve.

Consider children who are in an environment of constant change. Each year they experience a new teacher and classroom and possibly a new set of peers. Couple that with new subjects to learn and new problems they cannot solve without growth. Children must learn to navigate new social situations. Their clothing and styles change as they physically grow. They are constantly learning new sports, introduced to new clubs and skillsets. Why? It is the only way for them to learn and grow. Apply this mindset to a career.

Ways to Stay in Motion

Environment

I have seen amazing, knowledgeable, talented and accomplished store managers, running multi-million dollar businesses, stay in the same store too long, become complacent, and ultimately lose their jobs. These individuals did not create change for themselves. Change does not have to be a completely new job. Even an environmental change with the same company and position can be all that is needed to heighten the senses and renew interest. Moving a store manager to a new building, they can suddenly see processes that are not being completed correctly. They have a different team with different strengths. They can see clearly to refine processes, streamline staffing, and effect change. Interesting enough, those same issues may have been in their previous store but were no longer seen. Making a move creates a new perspective.

Within a Job

Sometimes change can be created in the job itself. If the job allows the leeway to alter the focus, the processes used to accomplish objectives, or any other aspect of the job, take advantage of that freedom and effect changes. Not just for change sake, but to better the company. If that is not an option, even small changes can boost brainpower. The important part is to create change so the mind stays alert, so interest is piqued. Here are some ideas to get started creating change:

 Drive a different way to work this week. Even this small change will perk up your brain and you may see things at work you could not see before.

 Try a new restaurant for lunch; in fact try a new food. Experiencing new tastes is good for the brain.

 Have lunch with someone from work whom you do not know well.

 List out your work routine. What can be implemented to enhance or change it?

 Come up with a new idea that will create efficiencies in the department, make a process better, create more sales, and so forth. If additional approvals are necessary pitch it to the appropriate person, if not – implement it.

Continuing to set goals is a way to stay challenged and growing.

 Try out some new software that can be used in the job. It could be software already owned just not learned or aspects of the installed software not yet fully utilized.

 For your next meeting use a visual aid not used before.

 Look at your workspace and see how it could be altered to create efficiencies. Clean out all unneeded stuff, put up new pictures or motivational sayings, redecorate. Create a new environment.

 List ten changes to implement in your current job or environment not outlined above. Choose three and implement.

 Ask a colleague to teach you something in which they excel.

 Seek out available training. If there is no training internally ask permission to attend a webinar, offsite seminar or workshop, or find training online for free or a nominal cost.

 Over the course of this next week, what other areas of the company interest you? Start making contacts and create cross functional learning. How can you integrate the knowledge into your current job?

Make Your Own Movement

Some companies and managers understand this concept and create the motion as part of the company culture. Others do not and it is up to the individual to make movement happen for themselves. If the current job has been mastered and a new challenge is needed position-wise, then get started looking at the possibilities.

Within Your Company

1) Look at the possibilities of positions within the company or department. Find three jobs/positions of interest. Look at positions that are open as well as those that are not.

2) Review the qualifications and notate any that require additional experience. Create a strategy to get exposure in those areas.

3) If appropriate, bring ideas and solutions to: the Boss, HR, Mentor, Director, VP, the President, whomever is appropriate, and get their thoughts. Are they supportive? Will they provide help? Many times goals need to be made known and then work towards them. Otherwise, a position may become available but you are not considered because others were not aware of any interest. Review time can be a great opportunity to have this

discussion, but don't wait if scheduled reviews are far away.

4) If the boss (or others in the company) cannot help, for whatever reason, don't let that be a roadblock. Figure out next steps and take action. The responsibility is yours.

There was a talented store manager I knew whose boss determined she would not be ready for promotion any time soon. In fact, she had been removed from any future consideration. Disagreeing with the opinion of her boss, she assessed her skills and began applying to positions in a different region where she did get promoted and was very successful. A perfect example where a person created movement for herself.

Beyond Your Company

The time may come when personal growth surpasses the ability of a company to keep up. Decision makers may be unwilling to grant additional challenges and opportunities. It is time to look beyond the current company for opportunities to grow. The same actions apply. See what jobs are out there and compare your skill sets with what is needed. Work to shore up any deficits, update the resume, and start applying.

If a leader reading this, understand you must give people challenging and interesting work which fosters their ability to grow in order to keep them.

Timing

How often movement is needed is different for each person. Some people need constant change in order to stay engaged and must create that movement for themselves. Others need to stay in the same place for a longer time period. But even for those that do not like it, movement is healthy and necessary in order to avoid becoming stagnated.

As a general rule, three years is the longest I suggest to stay in the same position/location. The first year is focused on transitioning and learning. The second year is the application and implementation of all the lessons learned. By the third year the focus changes to teaching and leading others and developing a replacement. That means it is time to move on, learn something new, continue to grow, and allow another person to move into the vacated position and perpetuate the cycle.

Is it Always Necessary?

Not everyone needs to move from where they are. If a recent change was made, a move to a new position, a promotion received, a new team to develop, any myriad of reasons, the best decision might be to stay in place. Some people have so much change going on in their personal lives that adding one more change professionally could propel them over the edge of being completely overwhelmed. I am not advocating that every person needs to move right now. I am simply championing the idea that, while the present role may be perfect currently, in time a change will need to be made in order stay engaged and thriving. Eventually, whether it be now, next year, or five years from now, give yourself the gift of movement.

Creating a Plan

Be responsible for growth and movement. If in a current role for over a year with a feeling of comfort, work through the exercise below to be pro-active in creating motion. Use the questions and example template to get started.

- ✓ What are your career goals one year from now? Three years? Five years? Create a new worksheet for each career goal.

- ✓ What have you already done that has created growth for yourself in your job? What were the results?

- ✓ What can you do to create growth, efficiencies, development in your current job?

- ✓ What do you want to experience, learn, grow within your current role?

- ✓ What do you see as opportunities in current processes you would like to implement?

✓ What are your strengths?

✓ How can you capitalize on those strengths to pursue stretch assignments, captainships, exposure in other areas?

✓ What are your developmental opportunities?

✓ What can you do to shore up those opportunities?

✓ What classes/seminars/learnings are of interest?

15

The Secrets of
Effective Game
Plans

If supportive, share the information with the boss and solicit their help as a partner in development. Decide what will be put into action, create a game plan, and make it happen.

Motion and Growth			
Name	Time in Position	1 1/2 yrs	Career Aspirations?

Growth Activities	Date	Result?

Strengths	Strength Assignments Ideas

Development Opportunities	Developmental Assignments Ideas

Responsibilities as a Leader

As a leader, it is important to create change for those reporting to you. If a talented and accomplished person is starting to be less engaged – help them make a change. Give them a stretch assignment, move their territory, help them develop a new way, switch up projects, create some developmental programs for them, send them to another department to bring back ideas to integrate into your own. Develop and grow your team. Part of being a leader is recognizing when others begin to stagnate and then create motion.

Summary

As humans, we need a certain amount of change in order to thrive, in order for our minds to stay healthy and engaged, in order for our brains to function at a high level, for our interest to be piqued, in order to grow. Movement can come in many forms: position, environment, challenges, it just needs to be new.

It is each person's responsibility to create motion for themselves. Only then will growth continue, not only in careers but as individuals as well.

Chapter Seventeen

Market Yourself

You Are Your Best Advocate

It is up to each person to ensure the boss and other decision makers have the right information at the right time. That includes what the individual is doing and how they are positively impacting the business. It is up to each person to create the perception others have of them. There will be champions along the way as well as detractors, but the individual is the only constant in their career and must take responsibility to take an active role in their own success. That means marketing: the act of promoting a product, in this case the individual.

The same basic principles of marketing a business apply to the individual. If potential decision makers do not know about the product, they will not buy it. If the decision makers in a career do not know what the individual has to offer, what their skillsets are, what they have accomplished, the decision maker will not buy the idea that they are at the forefront for consideration when deciding on a promotion, raise, stretch assignments, or other opportunity.

The boss and other decision makers only know some of what has been contributed. Even if working in the same building, ten feet away, they are not aware of everything accomplished. They have a host of responsibilities and focuses. It is up to each individual to ensure the boss stays informed.

As Regional Director I had ten district level managers reporting to me. All of them accomplished professionals in their own right, running huge businesses. Each was responsible for approximately ten stores. My territory included three time zones and five states which meant interaction with my direct reports was mostly via telephone and a quarterly visit to their area. I had a terrific team and when it came time for reviews it was tough to divvy up the finite amount of money I was allocated for raises and the percent of high scoring reviews. One individual had done a fantastic job on all the metrics, but I did not see anything above and beyond to put him higher than others that I knew had done many projects and helped outside of their districts. He received a good review but was very disappointed as he expected the highest possible review. During the conversation he explained all sorts of above and beyond actions he had taken, but unfortunately during his review was the first I had heard of these. It would have made a difference in his review had I known about his extra efforts prior. I wish he had been an advocate for himself.

Many have been taught not to lift themselves up, but to let others do it for them. They quietly help other people expecting nothing in return. In fact, many do it anonymously. That may work well in private life, but it does not work, as a rule, in work life. Waiting patiently in business to be "discovered" means a long wait ahead. Not that it never happens, but it is rare.

Effective Marketing

Effective marketing is not boastful but informative. People can only make decisions based off of the information they have at hand, and they will fill in the blanks with assumptions. Fill in the blanks for them rather than allowing the void to be filled with guesses. Communicate facts rather than allowing someone to use their assumptions in decision making.

A crucial part of business is information. The correct information at the right time can mean the difference in a company making it or going under. The same holds true for an individual. The correct information at the right time can be instrumental in positively affecting a career. As a boss, I appreciate when my team gives me information to keep me informed. I want and need it in order to be successful myself. Part of the job as employees is to ensure the boss, or other decision maker, has the correct data in which to make those decisions. Sometimes, these decisions have to do with an individual. When that is the case, make sure they have the right information to make the best decision.

There are good and bad marketing ploys, just as there are effective and ineffective ways to market oneself. Bragging definitely falls into the wrong category, although it can be effective. Hoping to get noticed is also the wrong way and rarely, if ever, works.

Bragging – A Short Term View

Bragging is typically facilitated by fear, insecurity, and competitiveness. This person is afraid if they do not bring up their accomplishments no one will acknowledge them, most importantly those in authority. Showcasing their accomplishments or abilities makes them feel more validated and may prove to themselves they are worthy of the position they have. It may be justification for their hard work or proof to others of their stellar performance. The braggart is hoping for validation and agreement from others. When they do not receive it they try even harder and brag even more, exaggerating their accomplishments for effect.

Unfortunately, bragging creates a loss of credibility as opposed to the anticipated gain. People begin discounting what is said. They brush off the braggart's real accomplishments, along with those that are surface, because it is hard to tell the difference. The person bragging may be labeled as arrogant and selfish. Others may not want to work with this person because they are not a team player. There is concern that any successes will be touted as the braggart's alone.

There is definitely a line between bragging and marketing. Bragging is to speak with exaggeration and excessive pride, especially about oneself. Marketing is the promotion of information in an effort to sell an idea, brand or product. But at the end of day, when all is sifted out, the braggart (if their work backs it up) actually has the advantage over the quiet worker. In the absence of any other information, the braggart is getting press and their work is being considered. The quiet worker may be doing a fantastic job, but there is no marketing to let others know about it.

It is easy to fall into the habit of being frustrated if the person bragging seems to get the attention, the breaks, or the promotions, when others are doing a better job. This is where marketing comes in. The key is to market in an informative way, to enhance the boss's ability to perform and have information at the right time. There are many ways to accomplish this.

Marketing Plans

Keep a List of Accomplishments by Month

I had a boss that required us to send him monthly accomplishments, not what we did in our jobs, but what we did above and beyond. At first, completing this list was just an irritant: one more to do item piling on to the already overwhelming work load. But as I did it, it not only helped me ensure I was actually accomplishing something above and beyond each month (even if it was small), it was also a great way to market and made my self-appraisal very easy to write. Most bosses will not ask for this, but it is a helpful list to create and have at the ready for the right moment to share. Creating a reoccurring calendar reminder can make it easier to remember and update the list.

Utilize Weekly/Monthly Updates

If updates are not required formally, then create them informally. No need to ask for the boss's permission to give him or her updates on the business. Each week or month, whatever interval fits better, update the boss on what has been happening, what has been done to solve issues, and any other information that is edifying. Utilizing an update process has many benefits:

- ✓ It is a pro-active approach to running the business

- ✓ It creates confidence being on top of the job

- ✓ Stays one step ahead of the boss in answering questions before they are asked

- ✓ Gives a forum to explain accomplishments in an informative way

- ✓ Keeps the boss in the know

Updates can be done face to face, via email or text, a phone call, or any other communication avenue the company uses. If doing face to face, leave the boss with a one page summary or email the list. It is great to keep the conversation on point, use as an agenda, and ensure all salient points have been touched upon. It also gives the boss the information both visually and by hearing to help with retention. Keep the emails or the meetings short; otherwise it will be difficult to get the information across.

Share Best Practices

Jump on the opportunity to share successes that can be duplicated and helpful to others. Make the presentation memorable, be seen as a team player, allow others to share in the success by duplicating the actions themselves, and impress the boss all at the same time. Don't just check the box off on this request, look at it as free marketing!

As a regional manager and director I visited stores every week, sometimes as many as ten. With a region of 96 stores and ten districts it was difficult to remember what I saw, who I talked to, and what to follow up on. I created a one page store walk checklist and notes page. I scanned all my notes once they were complete and had an electronic copy on my iPad with me for future use. This turned into a fantastic best practice I shared with my peers, was used by others, and gave me great marketing because I had a fantastic reputation for remembering, following up, and knowing what occurred at the walk. My boss and others saw me use it consistently. Here is a template of the walk sheet I created. Most everything is obsolete as to how Home Depot runs today, but it gives an idea.

Operations Walk   Date: _____

DM:	
SM:	
OASM:	
SASM:	

Walk Checklist   Walk Notes   Overall: ☐

Customer Service   R/Y/G

Maps
Clinic Board / Designated Area
Mgr Picture at exit
Coaches
Attrition
FT/PT
PK Certification

Likelihood to Reccomend
VOC Board
Yes, Empowered
Weekend Staffing

InStock

In Stock Condition   System   Store   Walk Count
OOS Board
Tags Updates / Overdue
Cart Adjst / Inv to Plan
Leadership Skus
DH Engaged / Work Opn Tub

Specialty

Spliy W/E Stfg
Splst SPH
Closed Quotes

Business

Sales vs Fcst
Payroll % to Plan
P and L

Action Items

Owner	
Flw Up Date	
Owner	
Flw Up Date	
Owner	
Flw Up Date	
Owner	
Flw Up Date	

Take Advantage of Self-Appraisals

Most people view self-appraisals as an unnecessary evil of working, hoping the boss or HR will forget to communicate that one must be completed. Most people stick to the barest amount acceptable to submit. Change the thought process and approach to self-appraisals. Use it to remind the boss of all the great actions and accomplishments achieved. Pull out the monthly accomplishments list as a reference and make sure to include every one of them in the self-appraisal.

There are three types of managers as it relates to utilizing self-appraisals: the negligent, the lazy, and the informed. The negligent manager will forget to read submitted self-appraisals. The lazy manager will read through a self-appraisal and as long as they basically agree, will use it for the actual review. The informed manager will read it during the review process to ensure they have not missed anything. No matter which type of manager, write a good comprehensive appraisal that includes all accomplishments. Turn the self-appraisal in early. Ask the boss to review it prior to them writing the final review and prior to determining ratings and increases. It can make a difference. Many companies do all the ratings and increases first, and then the managers write the reviews. Make sure all accomplishments have been considered before it is too late.

Create Your Own Marketing Campaign

Market Research

First, as in any marketing campaign, conduct market research. In this case, research the boss and answer the questions below and any others that come to mind.

✓ What motivates her? Demotivates?

✓ What is important to him? Unimportant?

✓ What does he value? Not value?

✓ What are her strengths? Opportunities?

✓ What is he concerned about? Unconcerned about?

✓ What are the challenges she is facing? What is taken care of?

✓ What venues is he most comfortable in? Most uncomfortable?

✓ What communication style does she respond best to? Least to?

✓ How does he communicate?

✓ What is her vision for the department?

✓ What are his pet peeves?

✓ What are her career aspirations?

✓ What are his goals?

✓ Include other aspects.

Depending on the relationship with the boss, clarifying and confirming questions may be asked directly. I would suggest starting with a couple at a time within a larger conversation and see where that leads. The boss may not be open to questioning.

Next, research how other people relate to the boss.

- ✓ What do they do that elicits a positive response from the boss? Why?

- ✓ What do they do that elicits a negative response from the boss? Why?

And finally, look at your own dealings with the boss:

- ✓ What have you done that elicits a positive response from the boss? Why?

- ✓ What you have done that elicits a negative response from the boss? Why?

Response Observations	
Person	Behavior
Responds Well/Not Well	Why?

Data Analysis & Strategy

When creating a marketing plan, audience preferences must be known. Analysis of the data helps to understand and create a strategy tailored to what they value. Analysis does not have to take long. Look for trends. Are there answers that keep coming up? Note that. Are there answers that just don't fit the boss at all? Note that.

Once comfortable with the research, it is time to create a campaign to market the product: namely you.

- ✓ Determine market venues. Where to market? In a meeting, on an airplane, during a break, on a specific phone call? Look back at the market research to determine where the boss is the most receptive.

- ✓ Determine data that will be shared. What is going to give the boss information that will enable them to do a better job, or be more prepared? What can be summed up quickly showing actions taken care of or completed so the boss is in the loop? What information showcases skillsets that also makes the boss look and perform better?

- ✓ Determine communication style or vehicle. What does the boss respond to best? Paper, presentation, email, in person?

- ✓ Determine when marketing will occur. Include an actual date. Be cognizant of what the boss has going on and when he/she is the most receptive.

It is a good idea to touch base with the boss or supervisor to confirm what has been learned through research. Depending on the relationship and their receptivity, direct questions may be appropriate. For others, confirming in a more subtle way may work better. For example, if research shows the boss prefers information emailed rather than printed, suggest emailing information then ask if there is an alternate way he/she would prefer it; this way the preferences are confirmed without having to ask directly.

Market "You" Strategy		
	Data	
Venue (location):		
Communication Style:		
Date:		
Follow up:		
	Data	
Venue (location):		
Communication Style:		
Date:		
Follow up:		

Implementation and Follow Up

Now it is time to implement the strategy and see how it works. Take a moment to determine the success of the marketing. What went well? What was effective? What needs to

Greater Application

The same process can also be applied to other areas; for example, if wanting a proposal to be approved, or trying to get funding. Any number of applications can benefit from a little research ahead of time. Know the audience and tailor communication to be the most impactful to what is valued.

be changed for next time?   Observe how the information was received and why. Adjust and update the strategy as needed and continue.

A Few Don'ts

Don't Brag

Check to see if communication style will come off as excessive, inappropriate, excluding all others to shine on you alone, prideful, and so on. When marketing, provide valuable information in the process. The recipient should walk away knowing more than they did prior to the engagement. If all they walk away with is how highly an individual thinks of themselves, the marketing has failed.

The other issue with bragging is people begin to tune out and no longer hear what is said. If a braggart – stop bragging and wait a little while before speaking. Usually people that brag are trying to get attention because they feel that no one is seeing their value. Unfortunately, the opposite is occurring. Stop bragging and use the previous tips to add value instead.

Don't Assume Work will Stand for Itself

Many times there needs to be an explanation along with the work. How did it come to be? What was your role? What was the outcome? What was the thought process behind it? Remember, if incomplete information is communicated, others will fill in the voids with assumptions which are rarely correct.

At the same time, don't write a dissertation on the background and expect people to stick around for its entirety. Keep it short and concise, a sentence or two, and then move on unless further questions are asked.

Don't Take All the Glory

Make sure when communicating to include others that had a hand in the success. It seems counterproductive if trying to market oneself, but it actually raises standing. It shows you are a team player, you value others, you do not create in a vacuum. All are very positive attributes. It also helps others to shine, you being a part of their marketing.

Don't Give All the Glory Away

Some people, in their efforts to share the glory, actually go too far and give all the credit to others. Make sure peers and others in authority understand your part in the success. If the idea was yours but others implemented, an example phrasing could be:

> *I noticed [explain issue] and had the idea that if we changed [fill in the blank] it might solve it. So I partnered with [fill in names] and they really made it happen.*

275

Another way to ensure the boss or other peers know who originated the idea is to partner ahead of time. Then when the project is complete it is already known who started it.

Summary

It is each individual's responsibility to market themselves. Another way to think of marketing is great, effective communication. When marketing with great communication in mind, the business is being impacted in a positive way by keeping the boss in the loop. Ways to accomplish:

- ✓ Keep a monthly log of accomplishments above normal job duties to share with the boss.
- ✓ Give the boss weekly/monthly updates of accomplishments, problems solved, and ideas implemented.
- ✓ Share best practices.
- ✓ Take advantage of Self Appraisals and write one even if not required.
- ✓ Create a personal marketing campaign.

Appendix

<u>Appendix</u>

Worksheets

Access the worksheets corresponding to the activities found in the book by visiting:

www.TangibleTools.com

Chapter One:
> The Golden Ticket Review

Chapter Two:
> Approachable Person
> Unapproachable Person

Chapter Three:
> Eleventh Hour Crisis

Chapter Four:
> Positive Brainstorm
> Pros & Cons

Chapter Five:
> Growth Potential
> Processing Feedback
> Self-Assessment

Chapter Six:
> Budgeting Basics Worksheet
> Budgeting Basics Excel Worksheet

Chapter Seven:
> Impactful Ideas
> Impactful Ideas Excel Worksheet
> Observation
> Pick Your Team

Chapter Eight:
> Immediate Options
> Long Term Options
> What Now

Chapter Nine:
> Idea Presentation
> Partnering with Colleagues

Chapter Ten:
> Information Checklist

Chapter Twelve:
> Which Are You? Quiz
> Which Are You? Tally Sheet
> Solution Matrix

Chapter Thirteen:
> Leader Positioning

Chapter Fourteen:
> Feedback Request

About the Author

With over twenty years of both corporate and small business experience, Anne is known for creating clear actionable steps for business success. Anne is recognized for her ability to employ a developmental leadership style, to break down complex issues into attainable solutions, and create process efficiencies. She is an accomplished Leader, Director, Analyst, Project Manager, Trainer, Business Coach & Consultant, and Executive Mentor & Coach.

Starting as an entry level secretary, Anne successfully worked her way up the corporate ladder of The Home Depot holding such positions as Flooring Buyer, Finance & HR Analyst, Regional Specialty Manager, and Regional Operations Manager, among others. She ended her Home Depot career as the Regional Director of Operations covering a five state territory of $3 billion in annual sales.

After leaving Home Depot in 2013, Anne founded AT Development & Solutions. Anne focuses on helping women be successful both in the corporate world (through the Tangible Tools brand) and as entrepreneurs. Previous to owning and running AT Development & Solutions, Anne was a co-owner of a restaurant. She is also the CFO for Point of Solutions and sits on the Board of Directors for Celtic Life & Heritage Foundation.

Speaker Bookings

Anne Tipper presents keynote speeches and workshops for corporate events. For more information go to:

www.TangibleTools.com

Feedback

Have questions? Want to let us know about an experience you had or share a tool or idea that has helped you? Contact us at:

www.TangibleTools.com